KINGDOM WAY

KINGDOM WAY

SCHARLOTTE CELESTINE

TATE PUBLISHING
AND ENTERPRISES, LLC

Published by Tate Publishing & Enterprises, LLC
127 E. Trade Center Terrace | Mustang, Oklahoma 73064 USA
1.888.361.9473 | www.tatepublishing.com

Tate Publishing is committed to excellence in the publishing industry. The company reflects the philosophy established by the founders, based on Psalm 68:11,
"The Lord gave the word and great was the company of those who published it."

Book design copyright © 2014 by Tate Publishing, LLC. All rights reserved.
Cover design by Rtor Maghuyop
Interior design by Jimmy Sevilleno

Published in the United States of America

ISBN: 978-1-63418-127-3
Religion / Christian Life / Spiritual Growth
14.09.08

I WOULD LIKE to dedicate this book to my family. My husband Jeff and our children Jennifer, Kevin, Christina, Matthew, Kodi, and Cheyanne, and all the pastors at Gateway Church and all the pastors on TBN for the word of God they share with the body of Christ and listening audience tuning in to watch. With special thanks to our family and friends for their intercessory prayers, having faith that God answers prayers and could and would bring our whole family to Jesus. I also want to thank our church family: Robert Morris and all the associate pastors at Gateway Church in Southlake, Texas, for their Spirit-led teaching of the word of God and dedication to making disciples of all the church members to spread the good news about Jesus.

To Jeff my wonderful husband who supported my efforts in writing this book and growing in the Lord. Who truly has shined in my life not only as my loving husband but also as my best friend. The Lord has truly preformed a miracle in our marriage. As we continue to surrender our lives and seek to be closer to Him, He has drawn us closer together in our unity of marriage. Things are so much easier when we learn to put God first in our lives and allow Him to direct our paths. We love our Lord, each other, and all our brothers and sisters in Christ, with LOVE being the key. Learning together how to be true ambassadors for Jesus Christ by loving people and sharing the gospel of Jesus with them.

CONTENTS

FOREWORD

THERE IS AN awakening coming upon the earth. It is an awakening of the saints who will inherit the Kingdom, and if there was ever a time when we need practical, down-to-earth teaching about the Kingdom of God, it is NOW! Scharlotte has written a book that is a powerful, practical manual for having and maintaining a personal revival. As you read this book, I believe that God will establish the strong truths of His Word in your life. It will not only awaken you, but inspire you to walk and reign in your newly found freedoms of Christ. However, I do want to warn you that as you apply these principles in your life, you must be ready to be transformed, because you will never be same again. You will leave behind a lukewarm religious mindset and be launched into a white-hot relationship with a loving God that empowers you for His destiny of your life. So get ready! Get ready! Get ready! Get set! GO!

Robert Corbell
River of Life Christian Center Rusk, Texas

OPENING PRAYER

Abba, Father,

I KNOW THIS book would not exist without the inspiration of the Holy Spirit. Thank you Jesus for sending the Holy Spirit to work in and through me to touch the lives of others and draw them to You, in order to further the Kingdom of God. All the glory and honor and thanks be to You, my Abba, Father. Thanks for loving us as Your children. Thanks for correcting us when we need correcting. Thanks for prying us loose from the ways of the world in Your gentle, merciful, and loving way, one layer at a time. Thanks for continued guidance in all our thoughts and actions and spoken words. Thanks for reaching out to catch us each time we stumble as we learn to walk like Jesus. And Father, I pray that this book inspires every reader to draw closer to you. Bless them with a new hunger for Your word, and inspire them to live the kingdom way. Open their spiritual eyes and spiritual ears so that they may all hear Your voice, draw closer to You, and fall even more head over heels in love with You! I love You, Father, I love You, Jesus, and I love You, Holy Spirit. In Jesus's name, I pray. Amen.

"Repent, for the Kingdom of Heaven is at hand!"

"Jesus"

INTRODUCTION

AFTER I RECEIVED Jesus as my Savior, which was an awesome and unforgettable event in itself, along with my salvation came a hunger for the word of God. It was like my view of the world had flipped. I felt like everything was new, and I was seeing the world with new eyes and hearing things in a new way. Everything I thought I knew didn't measure up to what I felt in my own heart. It was a virtual tug-of-war between my mind and my spirit as I was growing spiritually, being transformed by Jesus, and reading God's word in the Bible.

I kept on praying for understanding, and my heavenly Father kept broadening my view. Almost like peeling off the layers of an onion to get to the heart of it (tears and all). I was created to see "the big picture" in everything. I've always needed to know "why" everything works or happens the way it does. I catch on faster by asking all the questions that lead me to stepping back, connecting the answers all together, and looking at the bigger picture or purpose in what I am accomplishing. How it all fits together like a puzzle. Each individual person performing their job and working together with each other to accomplish a united purpose—I looked at Christianity the same way.

I prayed for understanding and then dove in with an urgency to learn, feeling way behind and short of time because there is an end-of-the-year inspection and the Big Guy is coming (sorry, I've been an inspector for almost twenty years). I started with reading the Bible, you know, "the owners manual from the manufacturer." I started with the New Testament first because Jesus was there, and then I went on to the Old Testament. What's funny is I realized Jesus was there too. I watched TBN preachers everyday on TV and learned a little something from each one, and I prayed for Heavenly Father to show me where He wanted me to be fed. At the time, we visited different churches, trying to find the right one where we fit in. My husband Jeff was working in the Dallas Fort Worth area at the time, and I was traveling back and forth on the weekends to see him. My mind said going to a church building on Sunday was inconvenient for my travel schedule, and my spirit said I needed to belong to a church family to continue being fed by God's chosen teachers. So I kept praying for a church.

In the meantime, during a couple of our family get-togethers, a couple of the kids introduced me to an incredible singer on YouTube by the name of Kari Jobe. She was like what I imagine, sounding like a singing angel from heaven. I was told she attended at Gateway Church in Southlake, Texas, and it wasn't far from where my husband was staying in Dallas, about fifteen minutes, depending on the traffic and construction and time of day. So one Sunday, my husband encouraged me to go, the kids told me how to get there, and I went on an adventure to find this church and hear Kari. What I didn't expect was what I would feel just by walking into that church. When I walked through the doors, I had an overwhelming feeling of "coming home," like I was meant to be there. When the service started with praise and worship, I closed my eyes and felt like God was so near I could just reach out and touch Him, and I raised my hands in praise of my wonderful and awesome Savior and Almighty Father, openly crying in surrender and thankfulness for all He had changed in my life for the better. Then pastor Morris delivered his message in a simple, to-the-point, easy-to-understand way that left me feeling that I had truly been fed with the word and wanting to hear more.

As I continued to travel back and forth to Dallas, my husband and myself started visiting Gateway on Sundays, and at that time, we were still seeking a home church to attend. To give you a perspective of where we were at in this search, let me say that our home was about a three-hour drive from Gateway Church in Southlake, Texas.

One morning, I dreamed I walked into the doors at Gateway, and there was a huge angel. He took up the whole hallway side to side and top to bottom. He was glowing brilliant white, and he was motioning with his hands for me to come in, like he was asking, "What are you waiting for?" When I woke up, there was the mind struggle again. My mind saying, *this is not feasible to join membership in a church three hours from our home*, and on the other hand, the Holy Spirit impressing on me that, *we belong there to be fed*. So I discussed the situation with my husband, and when I was at the church, I talked to one of the associate pastors at Gateway about struggling to find a church. He said if I had an obvious answer like dreaming of an angel inviting us to come to Gateway, then I probably should accept the invitation even if it didn't make sense to us at the time. He advised that it's not for us to know why God tells us to do things, but it's for us to follow what He says to do and trust in Him. So my husband and I joined membership at Gateway in 2011. I started attending classes at the church and online and started our own personal DVD library of Gateway teachings. As I fed on the word of God, my understanding kept increasing, and then the WOW moments started happening. I started experiencing breakthrough in understanding. I attended online classes in Freedom Ministry (you can find this at www.gatewaypeople.com) and developed a deeper understanding on who I was created to be and what it meant to be reconnected to the Spirit of God living with an eternal spiritual connection.

Learning to depend on God to provide (the kingdom way) and becoming free of being tied down or enslaved by the world's view of life, which is a dependence on worldly things to provide for my needs.

I attended Kairos, which is a two-day course that Gateway Church gives, centered on setting you free from past negative experiences. Reconnecting you to the eternal love of our Father and Savior by breaking inner vows, generational curses, and strongholds the enemy has established to keep us trapped in repeated sinful tendencies. Held back by feelings of guilt and condemnation, instead of free the way we were created to be. As we prayed in class together to be set free from different things, I was sitting there with my eyes closed and started seeing huge steel walls in my mind, and they began to drop one at a time, revealing images from my past starting with my parents divorce. I started crying right there like I was a helpless child again. Trying to understand and deal with what was going on and, at the same time, understanding the first wall that I built to protect my heart from pain. Then the wall came down, showing me growing up feeling alone because mom worked to support us which established more walls of self-protection in my heart (I don't blame mom. She was doing what she could to support us). Then another wall came down, showing my abusive, alcoholic stepdad. Watching him physically abuse my mom and brother, walking the line of perfection, not wanting to mess up, so he wouldn't turn his anger on me, and mom just took it (defeated in spirit and in bondage to fear). The walls kept coming down, showing me my life before Jesus. I hadn't realized until then all the inner vows and walls of protection I had built up to protect myself, and Father showed me I could give it all to Him because He was big enough to take it and He started healing my heart as only He can. I actually heard His voice speak to me for the first time, sitting right there and surrendering my past to Him. He said, "I am your Father, and you are My daughter. I have you."

And in every fiber of my being, I knew it. Needless to say, I do recommend the Kairos experience to everyone. It brings another level of freedom to your life. It's like pulling off the scar tissue on your heart, which hurts at first but brings true healing of the soul wounds. Not just putting a Band-Aid on to patch it but letting the Lord heal the wounds.

Then an even bigger picture started to reveal itself: The Bible wasn't just an instruction book anymore; it was a love story. Telling the story of a patient and merciful Father longing for the return of His sons and daughters and going to great lengths to prepare a way for them to return to Him and be reconciled. All so He can lavish His love and healing and provisions on them. To the extreme of sending His only begotten Son to pay the price for all our sins now and forever. Free to those who will accept Him, turn from their sinful ways, and surrender to Jesus. Oh, what love and peace are attained through that surrender and acceptance. Father showed me through scripture and teachers how incredibly and wonderfully we are made. Created to fulfill the purpose He designed us for. How everything is created from His spoken word by His will and design. If you break that down to science teaching, solid items, broken down to the smallest form or particle, are actually vibrations of sound. If you look at humans, broken down to the step before vibrating sound particles, you find a glue substance that holds the particles or cells together in particular groups, in order to form particular organs and systems, in order to perform specific purposes to sustain life. That glue substance is called laminin, and when looked at under a microscope, it is in the shape of a cross. Jesus is not only the word of God but also the blood of Jesus; His sacrifice on the cross for us, and our acceptance of Him, is what gives eternal life. What holds us together is a substance that is in the shape of the cross. That's a WOW revelation of understanding!

Each of us is uniquely His own design and created for His purpose, working toward the same goal through one Holy Spirit.

It gave me a whole new perspective and appreciation for people around me. We are different because we are designed for different purposes, but we are all one family working through and empowered by the same Spirit for the glory of our Father. Nothing but love for each other can exist from that perspective. Love is the driving force in the kingdom of heaven.

> For God so loved the world that He gave His only begotten Son, that whoever believes in Him should not perish but have everlasting life. For God did not send His Son into the world to condemn the world, but that the world through Him might be saved.

> John 3:16-17 (NKJ)

> A new commandment I give to you, that you love one another; as I have loved you, that you also love one another. By this all will know that you are My disciples, if you have love for one another.

> John 13:34-35 (NKJ)

> Jesus said to them, "You shall love the Lord your God with all your heart, with all your soul, and with all your mind. This is the first and great commandment. And the second is like it: You shall love your neighbor as yourself. On these two commandments hang all the Law and the Prophets."

> Matthew 22:37-40 (NKJ)

If we love each other, we follow the will of our Father. We naturally do not break the commandments out of love for each other. The law shows us how much we need a Savior, and when we are truly saved, the Savior fills us with such a love for each other that when He is residing in us, His love works through us touching others' lives. When we do slip up, we have a merciful and loving Father with open arms, just waiting for us to call out to Him to pick us up and dust us off and set us on the right track again. It's an ongoing process of sanctification (growing in divine grace as a result of our commitment to Jesus).

As we draw closer to God through seeking Him out in scripture and in prayer time, we start to see that what we have is a relationship with our Father and not a religion (a relationship is what we had in the beginning when God first created man). We strive to empty our lives of our selfish and worldly nature and let our Father fill us with His knowledge and grace. So He works through us for His purpose. It's okay to have scheduled time for fun and vacations and such, which in my book are necessary, but at the same time, we should also be good stewards of our time. In Matthew chapter 21, Jesus went into the temple and started flipping over tables, cleansing the temple to restore it to the house of prayer. We should follow His example. No, I am not saying go and vandalize a church. I'm saying our bodies are "the temple of the Holy Spirit." Do you have so much piled up in your lives, work, after work activities, social events, movies and television, and so forth that you can't make room for quality time with your Heavenly Father each day to pray to Him and talk with Him and renew your mind with His word? If so, it may be time for some table flipping of your own to reprioritize your life and get it back on track.

After all these revelations, came my point of inspiration for this book. It was April of 2012. I was practicing my "putting God first of my day" by waking up earlier and making time to pray and read the Bible and thank Him for all His blessings; then I quieted myself to listen for His still small voice in my thoughts. I always keep a journal, a pen, and my Bible beside the bed so I can write down any thoughts that come to mind, anything I hear the Holy Spirit is speaking. That particular morning, I started writing the thoughts coming to mind, and when I reread them, it was clearly an outline for this book. Spelling out the basics I had just come through in my own journey, and showing the basics people needed to achieve or advance in spiritual growth and learning a kingdom way of living life here. It was centered around Hebrews chapter 6. We confess to know Jesus, but we are not all feeding on His word and walking out the kingdom way that Jesus came to show us. Jesus said, "repent for the kingdom of heaven is at hand" and "follow Me and I will make you fishers of men." As we surrender and seek Him, He leads us down the path prepared for us. He calls for us to change our worldly ways and follow His example and seek Him for direction and answers to our questions because He has all the answers. So what are you waiting for? As you seek Him, you will find Him. Still yourself, listen, and as you hear Him, say "Yes, Father." Then do whatever He calls you to do in faith. Then watch as the answered prayers and miracles happen in your life and all around you!

BEGINNING YOUR WALK/RECONCILIATION

Nevertheless, I have this against you,
that you have left your first love.
Remember therefore from where you have fallen;
repent and do the first works.

Revelation 2:4-5 (NKJ)

AWAKENING

IT's TIME FOR an awakening revival! We are mighty men and women of God. Children of our Abba, Father! Jesus left us dominion and authority over all created things through Him. Why are we walking around in a defeated state instead of being "more than conquerors"? Where is our armor? Do we even renew our minds with the word of God anymore? The enemy (which is the devil) has been having a field day with our families because we are not suited up to battle him! We are defeated by our own lack of knowledge of the word of God (the truth), as God wants us to see it.

How can we save our families if we don't know who we really are ourselves? What does the word of God say about who we are? Until we truly understand this, the enemy can keep us beat down, confused, and grieving over the loss of things that have been destined by God to leave this earth since the beginning of time. It's the devil's nature to try to keep us in a weak and defeated state where he can wreak havoc again and again, and we are allowing him to have a victorious field day in our families. When will enough be enough?

What are we trying to run in our lives and how is it working out for us? When will we reach the point that we see it's not working "our way" and turn to the "One" who can help us? That would be Jesus. Who heals you? Who cleanses you of all guilt and condemnation? Who removes your heavy burdens and washes you clean? Guess what! The Bible has all the answers to these questions and more. It's not hard; you just pray for understanding of His word, thank Him for showing you what He wants you to see, and then open the Bible and read!

It's time to take it all back! Everything the enemy has taken from us. How is this done? *Surrender to the King!*

WHAT DOES SURRENDER MEAN?

Here's the thing about surrender and the lie the enemy uses to keep us from making the step we need to make to free us. You ready? We think that because we go to church and know Jesus is real that these qualify us as saved or surrendered, but are we really walking as a believer or wallowing in the secret chains of sin and bondage still? The devil uses fear and pride as powerful tools to keep us this way. He uses thoughts like *Well, I've told everyone I'm a Christian, and if Suzy sees me go up front to the altar, then what will she think of me?* or *I'm a tough guy. I can't be seen by the guys I work with and live around as someone weak and crying at the altar in surrender and bowing down! No way!*

This is exactly where the enemy wants you "in fear," "in bond-age," "in rebellion to God's plan for you," and "too ashamed and prideful to (surrender) bow down to your King." Oh, how Satan loves to keep people supporting the kingdom of darkness and how successful so many people make him. People in rebellion, in denial of the truth, and full of prideful, shameful, fearful thoughts. More concerned about what people around them think than they are about what God thinks. So who are they really surrendered to or, better yet, who are they a slave to?

> He is despised and rejected by men, A Man of sorrows and acquainted with grief. And we hid, as it were, our faces from Him; He was despised and we did not esteem

Him. Surely He has borne our griefs and carried our sorrows; yet we esteemed Him stricken, smitten by God, and afflicted. But He was wounded for our transgressions, He was bruised for our iniquities; the chastisement for our peace was upon Him, and by His stripes we are healed. All we like sheep have gone astray; we have turned, everyone, to his own way; and the Lord has laid on Him the iniquity of us all.

Isaiah 53:3-6 (NKJ)

HOW DO WE SURRENDER?

Jesus said to him "I am the way, the truth, and the life. No one comes to the Father except through Me."

John 14:6 (NKJ)

Just pray! Bow down to the King, and ask Him to come into your life and transform you. Repent of being a sinner, and tell Him you believe in your heart that He was born into this earth, died on the cross for your sins, was buried in a tomb, was raised from the dead, and now sits at the right hand of our Father in heaven. Let Him know you surrender your life to Him.

But what does it say? "The Word is near you, in your mouth and in your heart" (that is, the word of faith which we preached), that if you confess with your mouth the Lord Jesus and believe in your heart that God has raised Him from the dead, you will be saved. For with the heart one believes unto righteousness, and with the mouth confession is made unto salvation.

Romans 10:8-10

If you have an overwhelming feeling inside you urging you to come forward when the pastor does an altar call at the church, it's the Holy Spirit of God calling out to His child to come forward and surrender to Jesus. I have seen some people in such denial and fear of this calling that they actually grip the back of the church chair in front of them to keep from going forward to their calling and resisting the Holy Spirit. If they only knew that surrender to the King is such freedom!

HOW DO YOU COME CLEAN?

Read, believe, and follow the word of God. There are saved people all around us, dragging all kinds of baggage. Just loaded down and heavy laden. Full of worries, stress, unforgiveness, grudges, hurts, and fears. Thoughts we should not be having if we are focusing on God. Negative thoughts are one of the ways we are attacked by the enemy, and negative thought patterns are open doors for the enemy to continue his attack on us and weaken us even further. We need to seek what God says through His word and stand firm on His truths.

> For God has not given us a spirit of fear, but of power and of love and of a sound mind.
>
> 2 Timothy 1:17

> Cast your burden on the Lord and He shall sustain you, He shall never permit the righteous to be moved.
>
> Psalm 55:22 (NKJ)

> If we confess our sins, He is faithful and just to forgive us our sins and to cleanse us from all unrighteousness.
>
> 1 John 1:9 (NKJ)

> But seek first the kingdom of God and His righteousness, and all these things shall be added to you.
>
> Matthew 6:33 (NKJ)

> But without faith it is impossible to please Him, for he who comes to God must believe that He is, and that He is a rewarder of those who diligently seek Him.
>
> Hebrews 11:6 (NKJ)

Most assuredly, I say to you, he who believes in Me, the works I do he will do also, and greater works than these he will do, because I go to My Father; and whatever you ask in My name, that I will do, that the Father may be glorified in the Son. If you ask anything in My name, I will do it.

John 14:12-14 (NKJ)

My people who are called by My name will humble themselves, and pray and seek My face, and turn from their wicked ways, then I will hear them from heaven, and forgive their sins and heal their land.

2 Chronicles 7:14 (NKJ)

I sought the Lord, and He heard me, and delivered me from all my fears.

Psalm 34:4 (NKJ)

Come to Me, all you who labor and are heavy laden, and I will give you rest. Take My yoke upon you and learn from Me, for I am gentle and lowly in heart, and you will find rest for your souls.

Matthew 11:28-29 (NKJ)

In prayer, we ask God to search our hearts:

Search me, O God, and know my heart; try me, and know my anxieties; and see if there is any wicked way in me, and lead me in the way everlasting.

Psalm 139:23 (NKJ)

And when ever you stand praying, if you have anything against anyone, forgive him, that your Father in heaven may also forgive you your trespasses. But if you do not forgive, neither will your Father in heaven forgive your trespasses.

Mark 11:25 (NKJ)

> Beloved, do not avenge yourselves, but rather give place to
> wrath; for it is written "Vengeance is Mine, I will repay"
> says the Lord. Therefore "If your enemy is hungry, feed
> him; If he is thirsty, give him a drink; for in so doing you
> will heap coals of fire on his head." Do not be overcome by
> evil, but overcome evil with good.
>
> Romans 12:19-21 (NKJ)

God is faithful to show us what we ask Him to show us. When
we ask Him to search our heart, the Holy Spirit may bring forth
thoughts in our head of things we did that were against the will
of God for us or against His commandments. Once He shows us,
we need to confess these things to Him. Agree that we know we
sinned against Him. Ask for forgiveness and repent. Repenting is
actually agreeing to change your ways, to think differently about
the situation, and to turn from the sinful nature and go the other
way. Which should be Gods way or direction He's leading you to
go. Ask Him to show you in His word the truth of the issue you
are seeking direction in.

> From that time Jesus began to preach and to say, "Repent,
> for the kingdom of heaven is at hand."
>
> Matthew 4:17

Jesus said these words many times during His teachings. He
wasn't just saying to change our ways because the kingdom was
coming soon. He wanted us to change our ways now because
when we are saved, we become citizens of the kingdom of heaven.
Our bodies are the "Holy Temple" where the Holy Spirit of the
Lord resides within us. How we act now makes a big difference.
Are we acting like citizens of His kingdom? Jesus said, "The
kingdom of heaven is at hand." That is here and now. If we can't
follow His ways now, by loving each other, taking care of each
other, reaching out to the lost with kindness and mercy, and forgiving each other as He forgave us, then what is wrong with this

picture? Seems there is still much work to be done in a short amount of time.

Forgiveness is a very vital thing in our Christian walk. It is actually something God does and we participate in. We are God's vessels created for His purpose. The power of God, through His grace, comes to us and flows through us, but we have to let things go to keep the channel or river of living water open (flowing), in order to participate in what God is using us for. This is so we will be able to positively affect the lives of people around us. Unconfessed sins build a dam, blocking the flow of God's work in us. We are to forgive others, and ourselves, just as Jesus has forgiven us of all our sins. Forgiveness truly sets you free of a lot of baggage. It's an unloading of mental burdens that are taking up space in our minds and hearts. It feels unfair at times, but it is the only way to be released and restored.

> Then Peter came to Him and said, "Lord, how often shall my brother sin against me, and I forgive him? Up to seven times?" Jesus said to him, "I do not say to you, up to seven times, but up to seventy times seven.
>
> Matthew 18:21-22 (NKJ)

> And if he sins against you seven times in a day, and seven times in a day returns to you, saying "I repent", you shall forgive him.
>
> Luke 17:4 (NKJ)

What forgiveness is "not":

- Forgiveness is not denial. Saying, "It's okay" or "It didn't hurt." It's not pretending.

- Forgiveness is not repression. Saying, "I'm supposed to, so I did, but I don't really want to forgive."

- Forgiveness is not letting the person off the hook for his actions or letting them go with out consequence; it's surrendering them to a higher authority. God's forgiveness is complete to those who surrender to His Son, and His punishment is far worse than anything we could humanly accomplish. So why do we hold on instead of trusting in the true authority.

- Forgiveness is not forgetting. You don't have to become "friends" later.

- Forgiveness is not becoming a doormat. You don't have to continue allowing the negative action to occur in your life. Don't allow unrighteousness in your life. Seek God's direction.

HOW DO WE RESPOND TO HURT, ANGER, AND UNFORGIVENESS?

Unforgiveness leads to sin. We start to foster the hurt, and it builds into a grudge and even hatred and bitterness. This can be directed to others and even toward ourselves. You always wind up hurting someone with your secret sin. It causes pain to yourself and others. There is fear involved, and it threatens the comfort of our life. Anger just covers the fear we feel. Anger is actually a secondary emotion or a result of pain or fear (protective reaction). Anger is not sin itself. Emotions are actually indicators of our beliefs. They are responses to violations to our beliefs. The feeling of anger should motivate us to make things right. Our normal reaction is to want to bring justice or make people pay for what they did wrong and to cause revenge, which does not fix anything but does make you just as guilty as them. The process of forgiveness is not easy. The Son of man sweats blood because it was so hard. It is too hard at times to accomplish on our own, and we do need God's help to achieve it.

What can the Holy Spirit accomplish in us when we surrender it? First, we make the decision "I will live for the rest of my life with the consequences of what they did to me without ever blaming them." Think about what Jesus did for us. Forgiving our sins and our wrong decisions! Then understand that unforgiveness has had control over us, but when we decide to regain control by submitting to God, He will heal us. This action of surrender also gives the sinner back to God for Him to deal justice with them. God can take a wrong heart and make it right so they can realize what they have done. Forgiveness takes the sinner out of our hands and puts the sinner back in God's hands. We release them to God for His perfect will to be done in our lives and theirs.

WHAT ELSE DOES SURRENDER DO?

It allows for restoration and healing in us by addressing all the pain and unforgiveness caused in our lives. Jesus bore our sins and the sins of others. Surrender allows Him to heal us. In the old days, wine mixed with mire was a form of anesthetic, and Jesus refused to take it at the cross because He didn't want His senses dulled. He wanted to take the pain fully then, so He can take our pain fully now.

> They gave Him sour wine mingled with gall to drink. But when He had tasted it, He would not drink.
>
> Matthew 27:34 (NKJ)

As we take our problems to Him, He can take our pain and heal us so we are no longer controlled by what they did to us. It did hurt me, but I don't blame them anymore. I gave them to Jesus so He can heal me. It is a process and takes time. When it starts hurting again, say "I give it to Him so He will continue to heal me." Over time, it leads to complete freedom.

> Therefore if the Son makes you free, you shall be free indeed.
>
> John 8:36 (NKJ)

> If we confess our sins, He is faithful and just to forgive us our sins and to cleanse us from all unrighteousness.
>
> 1 John 1:9 (NKJ)

WHAT ABOUT IDOL WORSHIP?

The first time the Holy Spirit put the topic of idol worship on my heart, I was truly shocked! I don't worship idols, or at least, I thought I didn't until I learned what one was. When I thought about idol worship, I thought about big golden statues in the image of bulls and cows and men, in which people still bow down to today. These are idols, but the meaning of an idol goes much deeper than what we see with the natural eye. An idol is really anything that you put before God in importance. Anything you turn to, in time of need, instead of turning to God to meet your needs.

I use to be a big "stress eater." When I felt pressure at work with important dead lines. When I had to drive in big city traffic. You get the picture, life in general, when you're not looking at the world through God's perspective. When the Holy Spirit started revealing God's perspective through His word, I understood for the first time that I really was tuning to food for comfort instead of turning to God who is my provider, my shelter, my comforter, and my healer. Sometimes I would even voice my personal problems to my friends first instead of asking God for His perspective and answer. I was really turned around in my prioritizing what was important. Why would we not turn to God first when He is the One with all the answers?

> But seek first the kingdom of God and His righteousness, and all these things shall be added to you.
>
> Matthew 6:30 (NKJ)

Come to Me, all you who labor and are heavy laden, and I will give you rest.

Matthew 11:28 (NKJ)

We should be turning to God first with everything. Transferring our burdens to God first, giving thanks and praise to Him first before we start our day, going to Him first in prayer when we have troubles, giving Him thanks first when we receive blessings, giving to Him first with 10 percent of our income (tithe) so others can be blessed by what God blessed us with, and at the same time, helping to build the kingdom by drawing in the lost.

WHAT KINGDOM?

JESUS SAID MANY times, "Repent for the kingdom of heaven is at hand." We are not to wait for Jesus to return to start living the kingdom way. We should be living the kingdom way right now! The angels take notes of all our actions, words, and works everyday, and there will be a judgment seat of Christ that all believers come to and account for their works on earth (what fruit each one bears for the kingdom) both good and bad. That's why Jesus said "repent" which means confess your sins and change your ways! Repentance is not just changing our mind about what we decide but it's also changing the way we think or see things.

> Now when He was asked by the Pharisees when the kingdom of God would come, He answered them and said, "The Kingdom of God does not come with observation; nor will they say, "see here!" or "see there!" for indeed, the Kingdom of God is within you."
>
> Luke 17:20-21 (NKJ)

> Or do you not know that your body is the temple of the Holy Spirit who is in you, whom you have from God, and you are not your own? For you were bought at a price; therefore glorify God in your body and in your spirit, which are God's.
>
> 1 Corinthians 6:19-20 (NKJ)

Every kingdom has a king, and in ours, it is Jesus the King of Kings! All believers are already citizens of the kingdom through the new covenant God made with us through the sacrifice of His Son and our Savior Jesus (our atonement for sins). Jesus is the way into the kingdom through acceptance of Him and surrender to His authority as our King. In a kingdom, it's not about independence (relying on ourselves), but it's about dependence on the King who is our provider of all things. As a citizen of the kingdom, which you already are if you have accepted Jesus into your life, you take *everything* to the King in prayer.

> For our citizenship is in heaven, from which we also eagerly wait for the Savior, the Lord Jesus Christ, who will transform our lowly body that it may be conformed to His glorious body, according to the working by which He is able to subdue all things to Himself.
>
> Philippians 3:20-21 (NKJ)

What does *everything* mean? Seek His counsel first in all matters of your life. Seek His will and purpose for your life to accomplish what He created you to do. Give Him the first part of your day in prayer and study time. Ask His opinion on all major decisions in your life—job changes, house and car purchases, financial decisions, health issue. The list is never ending because it's in everything that we need His will for us. Put Him first in line to talk to when good things happen in your life. Put Him first in line to talk to when bad things happen and have faith in Him to provide. As you receive income into your house, give the first 10 percent back to His church to help with missions, outreach, feeding the needy, clothing the needy, and supporting the churches' operational needs and efforts to bring in the lost (this list could keep going on and on). Honor the Sabbath as a day to rest and seek His counsel, to renew your mind and refocus on His purpose. Attend church to receive vital instruction for living in the kingdom. The Bible is the *Orientation Book of Guidelines* for living in the kingdom way.

WHAT BATTLE?

We need to know who we are and where the battle is. One thing is sure, you will start getting attacked and challenged by the enemy the minute you accept Jesus as your Savior and are born again in your spirit. It's no mystery that you drew a line in the sand and chose a side. The enemy usually goes straight for the areas you are gifted or anointed in. The devil is already mad that you slipped out of his hands, but the last thing he wants you to do is reach others with the good news and lead them to salvation too!

The battle is really for control of your mind or thoughts. For new believers, it's easy to be attacked because we are not strong in the knowledge of God's word (truth as written in the Bible). He can attack us because we don't know what it really means to be a new creation in Christ. We don't understand all the truths God says about who we are yet.

> For though we walk in the flesh, we do not war according to the flesh. For the weapons of our warfare are not carnal but mighty in God for pulling down strongholds, casting down arguments, and every high thing that exalts itself against the knowledge of God, bringing every thought into captivity to the obedience of Christ, and being ready to punish all disobedience when our obedience is fulfilled.
>
> 2 Corinthians 10:3-6 (NKJ)

> Put on the whole armor of God, that you may be able to stand against the wiles of the devil. For we do not wrestle against flesh and blood, but against principalities, against powers, against the rulers of the darkness of this age against spiritual hosts of wickedness in the heavenly places. Therefore take up the whole armor of God, that you may be able to withstand in the evil day, and having done all, to stand. Stand therefore, having girded your waist with truth, having put on the breast plate of righteousness, and having shod your feet with the preparation of the gos-

pel of peace; above all taking the shield of faith with which you will be able to quench all the fiery darts of the wicked one. And take the helmet of salvation, and the sword of the Spirit, which is the word of God; praying always with all prayer and supplication in the Spirit, being watchful to this end with all perseverance and supplication for all the saints – and for me, that the utterance may be given to me, that I may open my mouth boldly to make known the mystery of the gospel, for which I am an ambassador in chains; that in it I may speak boldly, as I ought to speak.

Ephesians 6:11-20 (NKJ)

Since the battle we face is against an unseen enemy, the truth we believe in our head will mean the difference in success or failure. We still have choices to make about what we believe, the truth in God's word or the lies of the enemy (Satan). This is why it's imperative to read and know God's word. So when the destructive and condemning thoughts start flooding your mind, you can say, "Wait a minute, those are lies from the enemy. God says I am His child, and we are overcomers, and we are forgiven by the blood of the Lamb, and we are righteousness in Christ."

What then shall we say to these things? If God is for us, who can be against us?

Romans 8:30 (NKJ)

Yet in all these things we are more than conquerors through Him who loved us.

Romans 8:37 (NKJ)

I can do all things through Christ who strengthens me.

Philippians 4:13 (NKJ)

You are not your old self anymore no matter how much the enemy tries to convince you that you are in order to keep you in a beat down defeated state of mind. And all that in order to keep you from testifying about our Savior and bearing fruit for the kingdom. You have to know what the truth in God's word says, and you have to know who you are. Jesus came to reclaim His sons and daughters. We are not who we were raised to be, but we are who we were created to be by God.

> And I give them eternal life, and they shall never perish; neither shall anyone snatch them out of My hand. My Father, who has given them to Me, is greater than all; and no one is able to snatch them out of My Father's hand. I and My Father are One.
>
> John 10:28-30 (NKJ)

For years, I walked around feeling kind of lost, like I was missing something. I was always trying different things to fill that void. Relationships, food, shopping, and vacations were all temporary highs. Everything seemed to fall short and could never make me feel totally accepted and loved and purposeful like I really made a difference. Everything was all about me. What made me feel happy, what made me feel good, and what I accomplished and did anyone notice. I was hurt by rejection, and I was hurt by people's judgments and opinions. I was disappointed about things I lacked. I, I, I, me, me, me. *Then came Jesus.*

I was frustrated because I kept making wrong decisions and causing hurt to myself and others around me. But Jesus got a hold of me one morning. I was flipping through the TV channels, getting ready for work that morning, and my remote stopped working while flipping through the stations. I figured the batteries had died on me again and was listening to the person on TV as I put my make-up on, and it happened to be a TBN preacher that came on air. He was talking about having Jesus in our lives fills the void or emptiness that nothing else in this earth could ever fill. Well that statement got my attention! And he said it was as easy as repeating a few simple words and meaning them in our hearts. Well something came alive inside of me (I learned later about the Holy Spirit). I felt like every fiber in my body was humming with life. I felt more alive than I've ever felt, and I was thinking, *I know in my heart this is true, and Jesus can fill my emptiness!* And before I knew it, my feet had walked me into the living room, and my legs couldn't hold me up anymore so I fell to my knees in the floor and I started crying out and repeating the words the preacher on TV said, "Jesus, I am a sinner and I am confessing my sins to You right now. I believe You came to earth to take my sins and You died on the cross to pay the price for them and God raised you from the dead to ascend to heaven. I ask You to come into my heart Jesus and wash all my sins away and be my Savior. I surrender myself to You! In Jesus's name. Amen."

It instantly felt like hundreds of pounds had been lifted from me. The weight of all the guilt and filth was lifted. I felt like I was going to burst out into shiny rays of light all over! (Of course, that didn't happen, but it's the only way I can explain what I was feeling inside.) Overjoyed, overwhelmed, and truly and completely accepted and loved like I had never felt before. And it didn't stop there; when I got to work, I couldn't stop smiling. I had such a feeling of love for the people around me and wanted to hug everyone to show them. I imagine this is something close to what we'll feel when we reach heaven, only heaven will be on a grander scale. Like a huge family reunion full of hugs and an overwhelming love for one another. I later found out that the preacher that my TV happened to freeze on that day was none other than Billy Graham. TBN was running re-runs of his famous sermons!

The next incredible thing was, I had tried at different times in my life to read the Bible but couldn't really understand it. It just did not make sense to me, so I was a little intimidated about opening it up to read. I prayed, "Please, God help me understand the words in Your book and give me a hunger to learn how You want me to be. In Jesus's name. Amen." I don't know how to explain it to you other than when you are saved, God removes the veil from your eyes and brings you understanding of His word. It is a totally spiritual transformation in your understanding.

RECONNECTED

By reading His word, I started to realize all the lies in my head that I had believed, and I started to see the truth that God says about who I am.

> Therefore, if anyone is in Christ, he is a new creation; old things have passed away; behold, all things have become new. Now all things are of God, who has reconciled us to Himself through Jesus Christ, and has given us the ministry of reconciliation, that is, that God was in Christ reconciling the world to Himself, not imputing their trespasses to them, and has committed to us the word of reconciliation. Now then, we are ambassadors for Christ, as though God were pleading, through us; we implore you on Christ's behalf, *be reconciled to God.*
>
> 2 Corinthians 5:17-20 (NKJ)

At the time of our surrender to King Jesus is when we become reconnected with the Spirit of God. Jesus is the atonement for our sins, now and forever. He is our intercessor, which allows us to be reconnected to our heavenly Father and reestablish a relationship that was intended to be in the beginning. We were originally created with the Spirit of God in us, fully able to walk and talk with God. When Adam and Eve sinned against God in the Garden of Eden, the sin caused a separation of His Spirit from ours. Because of the choices man made in the Garden of Eden (the falling away of man from God), mankind is born with a sinful nature and a free will. There is a choice given to accept Jesus as our Savior or to deny Him. When we accept Jesus as our Savior, we are washed clean of our sins and reconciled to God (reconnected to His Spirit).

When we are reconnected with God's Spirit, there is no end to how He can set us free, heal us, give us knowledge and prosperity, and use us for the original purpose He created us to fulfill. The last line in 2 Corinthians 5:20, "be reconciled to God," is not just for unbelievers becoming believers. That's also for believers who have been drawn astray by worldly things (sins). God sees all and knows all. He longs for you to return to Him so He can shower you with His love and mercy and grace. And it's as easy as repenting, confessing to Him what you have done, and asking Him to forgive you and show you in your heart what caused you to go astray in the first place. Ask Him to wash you clean and transform you in Jesus's name.

> If we confess our sins, He is faithful and just to forgive us our sins and to cleanse us from all unrighteousness.
>
> 1 John 1:9 (NKJ)

> Jesus says…"whatever you ask the Father in My name He will give you."
>
> John 16:23 (NKJ)

> Likewise, I say to you, there is joy in the presence of the angels of God over one sinner who repents.
>
> Luke 15:10 (NKJ)

WHO AM I?

As I read the word of God and the Spirit revealed things to me, I learned that who I thought I was: Scharlotte, wife of Jeff, mommy, housekeeper, wage earner, fund raiser, and general multi-tasker— these were just my job titles. Who I am is a child of my Abba, Father, and an heir with my King Jesus.

When I started having negative thoughts in my head, it helped having a list of my favorite scriptures to speak out loud (confessing the truth) and to remind me of who God says I am and what He blessed me with. I call them my "fighting words." Equivalent to swinging an invisible sword at the enemy (a sword built for a true princess warrior!)

You are of God, little children, and have overcome them, because He who is in you is greater than he who is in the world.

> 1 John 4:4 (NKJ)

They shall be My people, and I will be their God.

> Jeremiah 32:38 (NKJ)

But when the fullness of the time had come, God sent forth His Son, born of a woman, born under the law, to redeem those who were under the law, that they might receive the adoption as sons. And because you are sons, God has sent forth the Spirit of His Son into your hearts, crying out "Abba Father!" Therefore you are no longer a slave but a son, and if a son, than an heir of God through Christ.

> Galatians 4:4-7 (NKJ)

Therefore submit to God, resist the devil and he will flee from you.

> James 4:7 (NKJ)

When you start understanding "who" you really are, you also start understanding about how important it is to read the Bible and to learn the kingdom ways. The Bible is the instruction book from the manufacturer!

As we grow as Christians, the Holy Spirit continues to convict our hearts of anything that displeases Him. When you feel the conviction of the Holy Spirit, just pray for Father to search your heart and as He shows your sins, repent and ask forgiveness, and He is faithful to do so. The more we seek Him and strive to stay in right standing with Him, the closer He pulls you into an intimate relationship with Him. We are all in a process of learning and growing and transforming. From the worldly view or way in which we grew up to the kingdom way or what Gods word says. Learning not only who we are (God's children) but also what He created us to accomplish for His glory. (Chapter 9 has more scripture on "who we are.")

WE ARE ALL BROTHERS AND SISTERS

Alright, we are back to Adam and Eve on this one. God created Adam, took a rib from Adam and made Eve, and the human race multiplied from there. Each person is known by God before they are even formed in their mother's womb.

> For You formed my inward parts; You covered me in my mother's womb. I will praise You, for I am fearfully and wonderfully made,
>
> Psalm 139:13-14 (NKJ)

> And He made from one blood every nation of men to dwell on all the face of the earth, and has determined their pre-appointed times and boundaries of their dwellings.
>
> Acts 17:26 (NKJ)

We are uniquely designed for His glory to serve His will and purpose which He created us for.

> For I say, through the grace given to me, to everyone who is among you, not to think of himself more highly than he ought to think, but to think soberly, as God has dealt to each one a measure of faith. For as we have many members in one body, but all the members do not have the same function, so we, being many, are one body in Christ, and individually members of one another. Having then gifts differing according to the grace that is given to us, let us use them: if prophecy, let us prophesy in proportion to our faith; or ministry, let us use it in our ministering; he who teaches, in teaching; he who exhorts, in exhortation; he

who gives, with liberality; he who leads, with diligence; he who shows mercy, with cheerfulness.

Romans 12:3-8 (NKJ)

God does not want mindless robots. He wants family, sons and daughters, and personal relationships with each of us. And how we treat each other on earth matters! They are not just someone who lost their house in a fire—they are your brothers and sisters. They are not just a family who can't find work to feed their kids—they are your brothers and sisters. They are not "just unbelievers"—they are a brother or sister facing an eternal lake of fire and torture! We are not promised tomorrow. We should be helping each other out now!

***What does the Bible say about the kingdom way of helping each other out and how we should treat each other? Not just when we get to heaven but here and now.

When the Son of Man comes in His glory, and all the holy angels with Him, then He will sit on the throne of His glory. All the nations will be gathered before Him, and He will separate them one from another, as a shepherd divides his sheep from the goats. And He will set the sheep on His right hand, but the goats on the left. Then the King will say to those on His right hand, "Come, you blessed of My Father, inherit the kingdom prepared for you from the foundation of the world: for I was hungry and you gave Me food; I was thirsty and you gave Me drink; I was a stranger and you took Me in; I was naked and you clothed Me; I was sick and you visited Me, I was in prison and you came to Me." Then the righteous will answer Him, saying "Lord, when did we see You hungry and feed You, or thirsty and give You drink? When did we see You a stranger and take You in, or naked and clothe You? Or when did we see You sick, or in prison, and come to You? And the King will answer and say to them, "Assuredly, I say to you, inasmuch as you did it to one of the least of these

My brethren, you did it to Me." Then He will also say to those on the left hand, "Depart from Me, you cursed, into the everlasting fire prepared for the devil and his angels: for I was hungry and you gave Me no food; I was thirsty and you gave Me no drink; I was a stranger and you did not take Me in, naked and you did not clothe Me, sick and in prison and you did not visit Me." Then they also will answer Him, saying, "Lord, when did we see You hungry or thirsty or a stranger or naked or sick or in prison and did not minister to You?" Then He will answer them, saying "Assuredly, I say to you, inasmuch as you did not do it to one of the least of these, you did not do it to Me. And these will go away into everlasting punishment, but the righteous into eternal life."

Matthew 25:31-46 (NKJ)

If you really meditate on this, you will see the bigger picture that we are the "temple of the Holy Spirit" that the Spirit comes to live in us when we accept Jesus as our Savior and surrender to Him. So, if He resides in us, He resides in all Christians, and what ever we do to help each other, we are doing to help Him. That makes it so much easier to lend a helping hand when you understand the depth of what you are truly doing. I will give all for Him, Who gave all of Himself for me, and love people as if I am loving Jesus directly.

And whenever you stand praying, if you have anything against anyone, forgive him, that your Father in heaven may also forgive you your trespasses. But if you do not forgive, neither will your Father in heaven forgive your trespasses.

Mark 11:25-26 (NKJ)

But love your enemies, do good, and lend, hoping for nothing in return; and your reward will be great, and you will be sons of the Most High. For He is kind to the unthankful and evil. Therefore be merciful, just as your Father also is merciful.

Luke 6:35-36 (NKJ)

Judge not, and you shall not be judged. Condemn not, and you shall not be condemned. Forgive and you will be forgiven. Give, and it will be given to you; good measure, pressed down, shaken together, and running over will be put into your bosom. For with the same measure that you use, it will be measured back to you.

Luke 6:37-38 (NKJ)

A new commandment I give to you, that you love one another; as I have loved you, that you also love one another.

John 13:34 (NKJ)

Let love be without hypocrisy. Abhor what is evil. Cling to what is good. Be kindly affectionate to one another with brotherly love, in honor giving preference to one another; not lagging in diligence, fervent in spirit, serving the Lord; rejoicing in hope, patient in tribulation, continuing stead-fastly in prayer; distributing to the needs of the saints, given to hospitality. Bless those who persecute you; bless and do not curse. Rejoice with those who rejoice, and weep with those who weep. Be of the same mind toward one another. Do not set your mind on high things, but associ-ate with the humble. Do not be wise in your own opinion. Repay no one evil for evil. Have regard for good things in the sight of all men. If it is possible, as much as depends on you, live peaceably with all men. Beloved, do not avenge yourselves, but rather give place to wrath; for it is written, "Vengeance is Mine, I will repay," says the Lord. Therefore "If your enemy is hungry, feed him; If he is thirsty, give him drink; for in so doing you will heap coals of fire on his head." Do not be overcome by evil, but overcome evil with good.

Romans 12:10-21 (NKJ)

Let every soul be subject to the governing authorities. For there is no authority except from God, and the authorities that exist are appointed by God. Therefore whoever resists the authority resists the ordinance of God, and those who resist will bring judgment on themselves.

Romans 13:1-2 (NKJ)

Render therefore to all their due: taxes to whom taxes are due, customs to whom customs, fear to whom fear, honor to whom honor.

Romans 13:7 (NKJ)

Owe no one anything except to love one another, for he who loves another has fulfilled the law. For the commandments, "you shall not commit adultery, you shall not murder, you shall not steal, you shall not bear false witness, you shall not covet," and if there is any other commandment, are all summed up in this saying, namely "you shall love your neighbor as yourself." Love does no harm to a neighbor; therefore, love is the fulfillment of the law.

Romans 13:8-10 (NKJ)

Brethren, if a man is overtaken in any trespass, you who are spiritual restore such a one in spirit of gentleness, considering yourself lest you also be tempted. Bear one another's burdens, and so fulfill the law of Christ.

Galatians 6:1-2 (NKJ)

And He Himself gave some to be apostles, some prophets, some evangelists, and some pastors and teachers, for the equipping of the saints for the work of ministry, for the edifying of the body of Christ, till we all come to the unity of the faith and of the knowledge of the Son of God, to a perfect man, to the measure of the stature of the fullness of Christ; that we should no longer be children, tossed to and fro and carried about with every wind of doctrine, by the trickery of men, in the cunning craftiness of deceitful plotting, but, speaking the truth in love, may grow up in all things into Him who is head – Christ – from whom the whole body, joined and knit together by what every joint supplies, according to the effective working by which every part does its share, causes growth of the body for the edifying of itself in love.

Ephesians 4:11-16 (NKJ)

Let all bitterness, wrath, anger, clamor, and evil speaking be put away from you, with all malice. And be kind to one another, tenderhearted, forgiving one another, even as God in Christ forgave you.

Ephesians 4:31-32 (NKJ)

Servants, be submissive to your masters with all fear, not only to the good and gentle, but also to the harsh. For this is commendable, if because of conscience toward God one endures grief, suffering wrongfully. For what credit is it if, when you are beaten for your faults, you take it patiently? But when you do good and suffer, if you take it patiently, this is commendable before God. For to this you were called, because Christ also suffered for us, leaving us an example, that you should follow His steps: "Who committed no sin, nor was deceit found in His mouth;" Who, when He was reviled, did not revile in return; when He suffered, He did not threaten, but committed Himself to Him who judges righteously; who Himself bore our sins in His own body on the tree, that we, having died to sins might live for righteousness, by whose stripes you were healed. For you were like sheep going astray, but have now returned to the shepherd and overseer of your souls.

1 Peter 2:18-25 (NKJ)

Finally, all of you be of one mind, having compassion for one another; love as brothers, be tender hearted, be courteous, not returning evil for evil or reviling for reviling, but on the contrary blessing, knowing that you were called to this, that you may inherit a blessing. For "He who would love life and see good days, let him refrain his tongue from evil, and his lips from speaking deceit. Let him turn away from evil and do good; let him seek peace and pursue it. For the eyes of the Lord are on the righteous, and His ears are open to their prayers; but the face of the Lord is against those who do evil." And who is he who will harm you if you become followers of what is good? But even if you should suffer for righteousness sake, you are blessed. "And do not be afraid of their threats, nor be troubled." But sanctify the Lord God in your hearts, and always be ready to give a defense to everyone who asks you a reason for the hope that is in you, with meekness and fear; having a good conscience, that when they defame you as evildoers, those who revile your good conduct in Christ may be ashamed. For it is better, if it is the will of God, to suffer for doing good than for doing evil.

1 Peter 3:8-17 (NKJ)

Therefore, since Christ suffered for us in the flesh, arm yourselves also with the same mind, for he who has suffered in the flesh has ceased from sin, that he no longer should live the rest of his time in the flesh for the lusts of men, but for the will of God. For we have spent enough of our past lifetime in doing the will of the Gentiles – when we walked in lewdness, lusts, drunkenness, revelries, drinking parties, and abominable idolatries. In regard to those, they think it strange that you do not run with them in the same flood of dissipation, speaking evil of you. They will give an account to Him who is ready to judge the living and the dead.

1 Peter 4:1-5 (NKJ)

But the end of all things is at hand; therefore be serious and watchful in your prayers. And above all things have fervent love for one another, for "love will cover a multitude of sins". Be hospitable to one another with out grumbling. As each one has received a gift, minister it to one another, as good stewards of the manifold grace of God. If anyone speaks, let him speak as the oracles of God. If anyone ministers, let him do it as with the ability which God supplies, that in all things God may be glorified through Jesus Christ, to whom belong the glory and the dominion forever and ever. Amen.

1 Peter 4:7-11 (NKJ)

Therefore humble yourselves under the mighty hand of God, that He may exalt you in due time, casting all your care upon Him, for He cares for you. Be sober, be vigilant; because your adversary the devil walks about like a roaring lion, seeking whom he may devour. Resist him, stead fast in the faith, knowing that the same sufferings are experienced by your brotherhood in the world. But may the God of all grace, who called us to His eternal glory by Christ Jesus, after you have suffered a while, perfect, establish, strengthen, and settle you. To Him be the glory and the dominion forever and ever. Amen.

1 Peter 5:6-11 (NKJ)

By this we know love, because He laid down His life for us. And we also ought to lay down our lives for the brethren. But whoever has the worlds' goods, and sees his brother in need, and shuts up his heart from him, how does the love of God abide in him? My little children, let us not love in word or in tongue, but in deed and in truth. And by this we know that we are of the truth, and shall assure our hearts before Him. For if our hearts condemn us, God is greater than our heart, and knows all things. Beloved, if our heart does not condemn us, we have confidence toward God. And whatever we ask we receive from Him, because we keep His commandments and do those things that are pleasing in His sight. And this is His commandment: that we should believe on the name of His Son Jesus Christ and love one another, as He gave us commandment.

1 John 3:16-23 (NKJ)

Beloved, let us love one another, for love is of God; and everyone who loves is born of God and knows God. He who does not love does not know God, for God is love. In this the love of God was manifested toward us, that God has sent His only begotten Son into the world, that we might live through Him. In this is love, not that we loved God, but that He loved us and sent His Son to be the propitiation for our sins. Beloved, if God so loved us, we also ought to love one another.

1 John 4:7-11 (NKJ)

Love has been perfected among us in this; that we may have boldness in the day of judgment; because as He is, so are we in this world. There is no fear in love; but perfect love casts out fear, because fear involves torment. But he who fears has not been made perfect in love. We love Him because He first loved us.

1 John 4:17-19 (NKJ)

WHERE DOES THE CHURCH FIT INTO THE KINGDOM WAY?

As we surrender our lives to Jesus, He starts a transformation in our lives. Changing us from the worldly ways we have lived to the kingdom ways, which are laid out for us through His word in the Bible. We should be reading the Bible each day on our own so we renew our mind (our way of thinking) with His word. We should also be attending a church that teaches from the "whole Bible" so we are fed by the teachers and preachers of His word. Pastors have a special calling on their lives to feed the children of God. They are led and gifted by the Holy Spirit to deliver God's message to His children and are held to a higher standard than most people.

And He Himself gave some to be apostles, some prophets, some evangelists and some pastors and teachers, for the equipping of the saints for the work of ministry, for the edifying of the body of Christ, till we all come to the unity of the faith and of the knowledge of the Son of God, to a perfect man, to the measure of the stature of the fullness of Christ,

Ephesians 4:11-13 (NKJ)

My brethren, let not many of you become teachers, knowing that we shall receive a stricter judgment.

James 3:1 (NKJ)

The mystery of the seven stars which you saw in My right hand, and the seven golden lampstands: The seven stars are the angels of the seven churches, and the seven lampstands which you saw are the seven churches.

Revelation 1:20 (NKJ)

Church is where we go to hear the word of God and advance in our understanding of the Bible and the kingdom way. We interact with other believers and encourage and lift each other up. The church is not just four walls and a preacher where we go each Sunday. The church is the body of Christ and the Bride of Christ.

For as the body is one and has many members, but all the members of that one body, being many, are one body. So also is Christ. For by one Spirit we were all baptized into one body – whether Jews or Greeks, whether slaves or free, and have all been made to drink into one Spirit. For in fact the body is not one member but many.

1 Corinthians 12:12-14 (NKJ)

Now you are the body of Christ, and members individually.

1 Corinthians 12:27 (NKJ)

How is it then, brethren? Whenever you come together, each of you has a psalm, has a teaching, has a tongue, has a revelation, has an interpretation. Let all things be done for edification.

> 1 Corinthians 14:26 (NKJ)

The church is where we recharge after a long hard week of work and errands. It's where we renew our minds with the teaching of the word. It's a place to be taught the word so we can share the word outside of the church. Fruitful churches should accomplish the following all or in part: saving–healing–setting free–discipling–equipping–empowering–and teaching to serve. As we attend church, we are learning His word and will for our lives and being transformed by it. We learn the Kingdom of God principles and apply them in our daily lives. In the way we treat each other and share the word with others. As we learn to walk this way, we are empowered by God to go forth and bare fruit for the kingdom. We also check our armor (building our beliefs in the truth of God's word). We strengthen our defenses to fight against the enemy coming against us. We encourage each other and lift each other up in prayer. We are being trained as ambassadors of Christ (the body of Christ is the church). Our body is the temple of the Holy Spirit where He resides. When we walk out the church doors, we are being sent forth to draw people to Jesus.

> Now then, we are ambassadors for Christ, as though God were pleading through us we implore you on Christ's behalf, be reconciled to God.
>
> 2 Corinthians 5:20 (NKJ)

> But be doers of the word, and not hearers only, deceiving yourselves. For if anyone is a hearer of the word and not a doer, he is like a man observing his natural face in a mirror; for he observes himself, goes away, and immediately forgets what kind of man he was. But he who looks into the perfect law of liberty and continues in it, and is not a forgetful hearer, but a doer of the word, this one will be blessed in what he does.
>
> James 1:22-25 (NKJ)

> Who then is Paul, and who is Apollos, but ministers through whom you believed, as the Lord gave to each one? I planted, Apollos watered, but God gave the increase. So then neither he who plants is anything, nor he who waters, but God who gives the increase. Now he who plants, and he who waters are one, and each one will receive his own reward according to his own labor. For we are Gods fellow workers; you are God's field, you are God's building. According to the grace of God which was given to me, as a wise master builder I have laid the foundation and another builds on it. But let each one take heed how he builds on it. For no other foundation can anyone lay than that which is laid, which is Jesus Christ.
>
> 1 Corinthians 3:5-11 (NKJ)

We plant seeds by speaking the word of God (in the language of love), and we water by encouraging and feeding each other with the word of God and God will bring the increase, using the Holy Spirit to draw people to Jesus. That's why it's imperative to learn the word of God and to live the Christ-led life by example. People outside the church should be able to see Christ in us and be drawn to Him. The freer we become of worldly or carnal things, the closer we will be drawn to Him and the more we are empowered by the grace of God through the gifts of the Holy Spirit. What Jesus taught us as He walked this earth is what the example of the church should be. His every move or decision was based on the will of His Father. To accomplish the purpose He was sent for in submission to Father's will. He walked this earth without giving place to sin, without sin hindering His walk, and He was filled with the full grace of God to empower Him to complete the purpose He was sent here to accomplish. He started out by choosing twelve disciples to teach the word of God to, and then He sent them out with His authority to make disciples in all nations, to baptize them in the name of the Father, the Son, and the Holy Spirit, to heal the sick and diseased, to cast out demons, and to share the word and draw the lost all to Him.

And He put all things under His feet, and gave Him to be head over all things to the church, which is His body, the fullness of Him who fills all in all.

Ephesians 1:22-23 (NKJ)

And Jesus came and spoke to them, saying, "all authority has been given to Me in heaven and on earth. Go therefore, and make disciples of all the nations, baptizing them in the name of the Father and of the Son and of the Holy Spirit, teaching them to observe all things that I have commanded you; and lo, I am with you always, even to the end of the age." Amen.

Matthew 28:18-20 (NKJ)

Then He called His twelve disciples together and gave them power and authority over all demons, and to cure diseases. He sent them to preach the kingdom of God and to heal the sick.

Luke 9:1-2 (NKJ)

Most assuredly, I say to you, he who believes in Me, the works that I do he will do also; and greater works than these he will do, because I go to My Father. And whatever you ask in My name, that I will do, that the Father may be glorified in the Son. If you ask anything in My name, I will do it.

John 14:12-14 (NKJ)

When will Jesus return? When the gospel is preached in the entire world. Will you help spread the good news about Jesus?

And because lawlessness will abound, the love of many will grow cold. But he who endures to the end shall be saved. And this gospel of the kingdom will be preached in all the world as a witness to all nations, and then the end will come.

Matthew 24:12-14 (NKJ)

Then He said to His disciples, "The harvest truly is plentiful, but the laborers are few."

Matthew 9:37 (NKJ)

PRAISE HIM BECAUSE HE IS WORTHY OF OUR PRAISE!

A church is also a place to praise God for all His goodness and to show our gratitude for all He has done in our lives. He inhabits the praises of His people. We praise Him before the pastor's message in order to bring Him into our presence so we are fed exactly what He wants us to receive. He will reveal in each of us exactly what each of us needs to hear and receive from the message. The more grateful we are, the more He gives us things to be grateful for (miracles/answered prayers). If we do nothing but complain about what He's blessed us with, then why should He give us more? We should be grateful for everything He has done, everything He has provided, everything He has brought us through, and all we are blessed with.

We don't praise and worship God because we are worthy to. We praise and worship God because He is worthy of our praise. Praising God also has another benefit. It drives the devil crazy. Here are more things to drive him crazy: when you fast in secret for spiritual breakthroughs and answers or direction, when you pray in the name of Jesus (believing in faith for the answers), and again, when you praise Him from your heart, giving glory to the King of Kings, the Lord of Lords, and our Abba, Father!

Fasting that pleases God: This is basically refraining from things that bring you pleasure for a specified time in order to draw closer to God and receive His direction (A self-sacrifice for Him in order to pull closer to Him). (Refer to Isaiah 58)

Anytime you feel attacked by the enemy, praise the name of Jesus. Start blessing in the name of Jesus and telling Him all that you are grateful for and sing songs of worship to the King. Then see how fast the demons flee from you. Keep a song of praise in your heart and in your mouth all day. If you keep good stuff coming out of your mouth and your thoughts centered on Him, there's not much room for negativity.

> Therefore submit to God. Resist the devil and he will flee from you.
>
> James 4:7 (NKJ)

> Enter into His gates with thanksgiving and into His courts with praise.
>
> Psalm 100:4 (NKJ)

> Be anxious for nothing, but in every thing by prayer and supplication, with thanksgiving, let your requests be made known to God.
>
> Philippians 4:6 (NKJ)

> Make a joyful shout to God, all the earth! Sing out the honor of His name; make His praise glorious. Say to God, "How awesome are Your works! Through the greatness of Your power Your enemies shall submit themselves to You. All the earth shall worship You and sing praises to You; they shall sing praises to Your name." Come and see the works of God; He is awesome in His doing toward the sons of men. He turned the sea into dry land; they went through the river on foot. There we will rejoice in Him. He rules by His power forever; His eyes observe the nations; do not let the rebellious exalt themselves. Oh bless our God, you peoples! And make the voice of His praise to be heard, Who keeps our soul among the living, and does not allow our feet to be moved. For You, O God, have tested us; You have refined us as silver is refined. You brought us into the net; You laid affliction on our backs. You have caused men to ride over our heads; we went through fire and through water; but You brought us out to rich fulfillment.
>
> Psalm 66:1-12 (NKJ)

Raise your hands to the Lord in praise!

R—reach your hands to the Lord
A—ask the Lord for what you need (wisdom, healing, direction, etc.)
I—invite the Lord's presence into the situation you face
S—surrender yourself to the Lord and surrender your situation
E—embrace the Lord's promise (having faith, receiving His truth)

LIST OF QUIET KILLERS

Pay close attention to the following three items. They will sneak up on you when you least expect. That's why it is so important to stay in God's word each day so you continue to renew your mind with the kingdom way of thinking. Focus on God and His word, and you will learn to recognize the enemy's sneak attack when it comes at you.

1. *Bitterness and Sarcasm.* Saying things like, "they got what they deserved" or "they had it coming." We try to justify our statements and feelings by saying things like, "After all I did for them, look how they treated me!" (These are dangerous roots and poisonous fruits.) Having the grace of God, you should forgive them, and when you give or loan something, do so not expecting in return.

   But if you do not forgive, neither will your Father in heaven forgive our trespasses.

   Mark 11:26 (NKJ)

   But love your enemies, do good, and lend, hoping for nothing in return; and your reward will be great, and you will be sons of the Most High. For He is kind to the unthankful and evil. Therefore be merciful, just as your Father also is merciful.

   Luke 6:35-36 (NKJ)

2. *Worry.* By not trusting our troubles to God, we cause worry in our lives. We also cause worry and stress in our lives by taking on too much instead of praying about things before we agree to them. Are we trusting in the Lord and all the truths of His word, or are we believing what the enemy is trying to destroy us with?

Trust in the Lord with all your heart, and lean not on your own understanding.

Proverbs 3:5 (NKJ)

And do not seek what you should eat or what you should drink, nor have an anxious mind. For all these things the nations of the world seek after and Your Father knows that you need these things. But seek the kingdom of God, and all these things shall be added to you.

Luke 12:29-31 (NKJ)

3. *Anger.* This includes frustration, impatience, spewers of words in expression, and stewers of words in suppression.

A fool vents all his feelings, but a wise man holds them back.

Proverbs 29:11 (NKJ)

When I kept silent, my bones grew old, through my groaning all day long.

Psalm 32:3 (NKJ)

Be angry but do not sin "do not let the sun go down on your wrath, nor give place to the devil.

Ephesians 4:26-27 (NKJ)

Let all bitterness, wrath, anger, clamor, and evil speaking be put away from you with all malice. And be kind to one another, tender hearted, forgiving one another, even as God in Christ forgave you.

Ephesians 4:31 (NKJ)

When you face these three tactics of the enemy, remember the following scriptures:

> The thief does not come except to steal, and to kill and to destroy. I have come that they may have life, and that they may have it more abundantly.
>
> John 10:10 (NKJ)

> Therefore be imitators of God as dear children. And walk in love, as Christ also has loved us, and given Himself for us, an offering and a sacrifice to God for a sweet smelling aroma.
>
> Ephesians 5:1 (NKJ)

> Speaking of one another in psalms and hymns, and spiritual songs, singing and making melody in your heart to God, giving thanks always for all things to God the Father in the name of our Lord Jesus Christ, submitting to one another in the fear of God.
>
> Ephesians 5:19-21 (NKJ)

> But seek first the kingdom of God and His righteousness and all things shall be added to you.
>
> Matthew 6:33 (NKJ)

> He who says he abides in Him ought himself also to walk just as He walked.
>
> 1 John 2:6 (NKJ)

WAYS WE QUENCH THE HOLY SPIRIT

The Holy Spirit works the power of God through us. He leads and guides us, revealing the greater truths about Jesus through our diligent study of His word. It's not a good idea to do things to cause Him grief. We need His help, and He wants to be our friend and help us.

> However, when He, the Spirit of truth, has come, He will guide you into all truth; for He will not speak on His own authority, but whatever He hears He will speak; and He will tell you things to come. He will glorify Me, for He will take of what is Mine and declare it to you.
>
> John 16:13-14 (NKJ)

1. *Fear.* Being afraid of things in the world or scared of failure. This is *lack of faith* in God in whom we are to trust.

> Have I not commanded you? Be strong and of good courage; do not be afraid, nor be dismayed, for the Lord your God is with you wherever you go.
>
> Joshua 1:9 (NKJ)

> There is no fear in love; but perfect love casts out fear, because fear involves torment. But he who fears has not been made perfect in love.
>
> 1 John 4:18 (NKJ)

> But He said to them, "Why are you so fearful? How is it that you have no faith?"
>
> Mark 4:40 (NKJ)

> So he answered, "Do not fear, for those who are with us are more than those who are with them."
>
> 2 Kings 6:16 (NKJ)

> And do not fear those who kill the body but cannot kill the soul. But rather fear Him who is able to destroy both soul and body in hell.
>
> Matthew 10:28 (NKJ)

2. *Doubt and Unbelief* (No Faith)

> But without faith it is impossible to please Him, for he who comes to God must believe that He is, and that He is a rewarder of those who diligently seek Him.
>
> Hebrews 11:6 (NKJ)

> Let us draw near with a true heart in full assurance of faith, having our hearts sprinkled from an evil conscience and our bodies washed with pure water. Let us hold fast the confession of our hope without wavering, for He who promised is faithful.
>
> Hebrews 10:22-23 (NKJ)

3. *Grabbing the Glory.* This comes from selfishness by not giving the credit to God. Being prideful and drawing recognition to ourselves.

> Trust in the Lord with all your heart, and lean not on your own understanding; In all your ways acknowledge Him and He shall direct your paths.
>
> Proverbs 3:5-6 (NKJ)

> And whatever you do in word or deed, do all in the name of the Lord Jesus, giving thanks to God the Father through Him.
>
> Colossians 3:17 (NKJ)

4. *Disobedience, Habitual Sin, and Rebelliousness.* Knowing God's word and choosing to do what you want to regardless. ***A curse is a consequence of disobedience or rebellion, and curses have been broken by Jesus and still can be broken by Jesus. You should not only confess your sins but also confess the sins and the iniquities of your ancestors (generational curses). And Jesus is faithful to set us free.

You shall not bow down to them nor serve them. For I, the Lord your God, am a jealous God, visiting the iniquity of the fathers upon the children to the third and forth generations of those who hate Me, but showing mercy to thousands, to those who love Me and keep My commandments.

Exodus 20:5 (NKJ)

But He was wounded for our transgressions, He was bruised for our iniquities; the chastisement for our peace was upon Him, and by His stripes we are healed.

Isaiah 53:5 (NKJ)

Christ has redeemed us from the curse of the law, having become a curse for us (for it is written, "cursed is everyone who hangs on a tree.")

Galatians 3:13 (NKJ)

But if they confess their iniquity and the iniquity of their fathers, with their unfaithfulness in which they were unfaithful to Me, and that they also have walked contrary to Me, and that I also have walked contrary to them and have brought them into the land of their enemies; if their uncircumcised hearts are humbled, and they accept their guilt – then I will remember My covenant with Jacob, and My covenant with Isaac and My covenant with Abraham I will remember; I will remember the land.

Leviticus 26:40-42 (NKJ)

Then Jesus said to those Jews who believed Him, " If you abide in My word, you are My disciples indeed. And you shall know the truth, and the truth shall make you free."

John 8:31-32 (NKJ)

5. *Not Being Reconciled*. When you stop asking for forgiveness, He stops forgiving you, and you get farther from Him. Think about this, He sees all and knows all. Some

of you stop confessing your sin because you think God is tired of hearing it or you think the sin is too bad for Him to forgive. But what are you really saying? That what Jesus did on the cross for us was not enough?

If we confess our sins, He is faithful and just to forgive us our sins and to cleanse us from all unrighteousness.

1 John 1:9 (NKJ)

The Lord is not slack concerning His promise, as some count slackness, but is longsuffering towards us, not willing that any should perish but that all should come to repentance.

2 Peter 3:9 (NKJ)

Now all things are of God, who has reconciled us to Himself through Jesus Christ, and has given us the ministry of reconciliation, that is, that God was in Christ reconciling the world to Himself, not imputing their trespasses to them, and has committed to us the word of reconciliation.

2 Corinthians 5:18-19 (NKJ)

THE LORD'S CHASTENING

The word chastening (not chastising) means to give correction, not punishment. God's chastening is correcting our wrong behavior and is done because He loves us as our Father. He wants us to repent, change our ways, and learn to make right decisions based on His will for us. Jesus already took our chastisement on the cross. He paid the price for all our sins in the past, present, and future. Father does to each "as they deserve" (justice) not to each "the same" (fairness) when it comes to correction. Acting out against God's correction is rebellion and brings more or continued chastening. He is longsuffering. So the sooner we submit to His will and repent and return to Him, the sooner we are forgiven. His correcting is loving, not punitive. Stop justifying your wrong actions and agree with God as He shows you your sin, and He is faithful to forgive.

> If we confess our sins, He is faithful and just to forgive us our sins and to cleanse us from all unrighteousness.
>
> 1 John 1:9 (NKJ)

> My son, do not despise the chastening of the Lord, nor detest His correction; for whom the Lord loves He corrects, just as a father the son in whom he delights.
>
> Proverbs 3:11-12 (NKJ)

> If you endure chastening, God deals with you as with sons; for what son is there whom a father does not chasten? But if you are without chastening, of which all have become partakers, then you are illegitimate and not sons. Furthermore, we have had human fathers who corrected us, and we paid them respect. Shall we not much more readily be in subjection to the Father of spirits and live? For they indeed for a few days chastened us as seemed best to them, but He for our profit, that we may be partakers of His holiness. Now no chastening seems to be joyful for the present, but painful; never the less, afterward it yields the peaceable fruit of righteousness to those who have been trained by it.
>
> Hebrews 12:7-11 (NKJ)

TRIALS AND TRIBULATIONS

> Beloved, do not think it strange concerning the fiery trial which is to try you, as though some strange thing happened to you; but rejoice to the extent that you partake of Christ's sufferings, that when His glory is revealed, you may also be glad with exceeding joy.
>
> 1 Peter 4:12-13 (NKJ)

Therefore let those who suffer according to the will of God commit their souls to Him in doing good, as to a faithful Creator.

1 Peter 4:19 (NKJ)

My brethren, count it all joy when you fall into various trials, knowing that the testing of your faith produces patience. But let patience have its perfect work, that you may be perfect and complete, lacking nothing.

James 1:2-4 (NKJ)

Blessed is the man who endures temptation; for when he has been approved, he will receive the crown of life which the Lord has promised to those who love Him.

James 1:12 (NKJ)

It's not our job to know why we are suffering trials. It's our job to trust God in the midst of our suffering. All the while lifting our troubles up to Him in prayer, thanking Him for our provisions, and knowing that all things will work out to our good.

And we know that all things work together for good to those who love God to those who are the called according to His purpose.

Matthew 8:28 (NKJ)

Blessed be the God and Father of our Lord Jesus Christ, the Father of mercies and God of all comfort, who comforts us in all our tribulation, that we may be able to comfort those who are in any trouble, with the comfort with which we ourselves are comforted by God. For as the sufferings of Christ abound in us, so our consolation also abounds through Christ. Now if we are afflicted, it is for your consolation and salvation, which is effective for enduring the same sufferings which we also suffer. Or if we are comforted, it is for your consolation and salvation. And our hope for you is steadfast, because we know that as you are partakers of the sufferings, so also you will partake of the consolation.

2 Corinthians 1:3-7 (NKJ)

Yet in all these things we are more than conquerors through Him who loved us.

Romans 8:37 (NKJ)

No temptation has over taken you except such as is common to man; but God is faithful, who will not allow you to be tempted beyond what you are able, but with the temptation will also make the way of escape, that you may be able to bear it.

1 Corinthians 10:13 (NKJ)

For if we would judge ourselves, we would not be judged. But when we are judged, we are chastened by the Lord, that we may not be condemned with the world.

1 Corinthians 11:31-32 (NKJ)

***Do not let fear block your faith!

But He was in the stern, asleep on a pillow, and they awoke Him and said, "Teacher, do you not care that we are perishing?" Then He arose and rebuked the wind and said to the sea, "Peace, be still," and the wind ceased and there was great calm. But He said to them, "Why are you so fearful? How is it that you have no faith?"

Mark 4:38 (NKJ)

Jesus did not rebuke them for disturbing Him with their prayers, but He rebuked them for disturbing themselves with their fears (lack of faith). Fear hurts the heart of Jesus because fear is the greatest insult that a believer can give God. The purpose of storms in our lives is so we will turn to God and put our faith in Him. He hears our prayers because we put our trust in Him.

Purpose of storms:

- To learn to defeat fear.
- To increase faith.
- To bring glory to God.

We pray and worship to God through our storms in order to get our focus off the storm and back on God.

DRAWING CLOSER

PRAYER OF INTERCESSION

JESUS IS INTERCEDING for us. Intercession is not a prayer but a work. It's what Jesus does when we pray in faith. Faith is our part. It's believing and trusting in what Jesus can do. Intercession is to bring two together. Jesus represents us to our Father. He pleads our case, and furthermore, when we couldn't reach God, God reached us with an intercessor, Jesus! Jesus is the bridge between us and God. We have a Savior who humbled Himself to be born in the flesh and walk in the flesh and be tempted in the flesh. He knows what challenges we face each day on this earth.

> For we do not have a High Priest who cannot sympathize with our weaknesses, but was in all points tempted as we are, yet without sin.
>
> Hebrews 4:15 (NKJ)

> Who is he who condemns? It is Christ who died, and furthermore is also risen, who is even at the right hand of God, who also makes intercession for us.
>
> Romans 8:34 (NKJ)

Therefore He is also able to save to the uttermost those who come to God through Him, since He always lives to make intercession for them.

Hebrews 7:25 (NKJ)

Therefore I will divide Him a portion with the great, and He shall divide the spoil with the strong, because He poured out His soul unto death, and He was numbered with the transgressors, and He bore the sin of many, and made intersession for the transgressors.

Isaiah 53:12 (NKJ)

THE HOLY SPIRIT INTERCEDES

Likewise the Spirit also helps in our weakness. For we do not know what we should pray for as we ought, but the Spirit Himself makes intercession for us with groaning which cannot be uttered.

Romans 8:26 (NKJ)

Ask the Holy Spirit to pray what the will of God is for our lives. The Holy Spirit will pray to the mind of God for us. Prayer is a way of transferring our burden to God and trust (have faith) that His perfect will in that situation will be done. He knows the heart of every man, and He knows the purpose He is working in each one of our lives. He is the Creator of all, and He sees all and knows all. The farthest we can carry any burden is to the feet of Jesus. Lay your troubles at the cross, and trust that what Jesus accomplished for us is enough. When we pray, the Holy Spirit will also bring things to mind for us to pray about. He will lead you in the direction to go in prayer to intercede for different people and topics, and then the Holy Spirit carries it to the Father. That's why it's always good to pray something like:

"Father, what is your will in _____ situation?" and "Father, your perfect will be done in the life of _____, on earth as it is in heaven. In Jesus's name. Amen".

WE SHOULD ALSO BE INTERCEDING

Jesus reached down to us when we could not reach Him. We should be standing in the gap for people around us. First off, bring your will into submission or agreement with God's will. Ask for His presence in prayer and thank Him. Tell Him all you are grateful for and that all the glory and honor and thanksgiving are to Him. Take people that are on your heart to Him, and pray His perfect will be done in their lives. Thank Him again for all He is manifesting in our lives and the lives of those we are praying for. In Jesus's name, I pray. Amen.

> Therefore I exhort first of all that supplications, prayers, intercessions and giving of thanks be made for all men, for kings, and all who are in authority, that we may lead a quiet and peaceable life in all godliness and reverence.
>
> 1 Timothy 2:1-2 (NKJ)

THE PRAYER OF POWER

God has deposited His power in us!

> Behold, I send the Promise of My Father upon you; but tarry in the city of Jerusalem until you are endued with power from on high.
>
> Luke 24:49 (NKJ)

> But you shall receive power when the Holy Spirit has come upon you; and you shall be witnesses to Me in Jerusalem, and in all Judea and Samaria, and to the end of the earth.
>
> Acts 1:8 (NKJ)

> Now to Him who is able to do exceedingly abundantly above all that we ask or think, according to the power that works in us,
>
> Ephesians 3:20 (NKJ)

I have made the earth, the man and the beast that are on the ground, by My great power and by My outstretched arm, and have given it to whom it seemed proper to Me.

Jeremiah 27:5 (NKJ)

God's unlimited power is also released through the prayers of His people. Is the power of God a river or a trickle in your lives?

On the last day, the great day of the feast, Jesus stood and cried out, "If anyone thirsts, let him come to Me and drink. He who believes in Me, as the scripture has said, out of his heart will flow rivers of living water." But this He spoke concerning the Spirit, whom those believing in Him would receive; for the Holy Spirit was not yet given, because Jesus was not yet glorified.

John 7:37-39 (NKJ)

God has given the stewardship of our life to us. We should be praying and seeking God's will for answered prayers. God's will for each one of us is for us to repent as He shows us areas of sin in our life. He wants to change our worldly ways to the way of the kingdom of heaven as Jesus taught when He was here walking with His disciples and teaching the multitudes.

During times of need in our lives, when we need God to answer prayers in situations we view as serious, we should pull back from worldly things and pull closer to God for answers. We should read the Bible, pray, and even fast from things that normally distract us. Such as TV, computers, movies, eating out, shopping, or even fast from certain favorite foods (like sugar and desserts). There are many books out on safe ways to fast from foods.

And you will seek Me and find Me, when you search for Me with all your heart.

Jeremiah 29:13 (NKJ)

WHAT ARE SOME OF THE REASONS WHY WE DON'T PRAY

Complacency. We just don't work it into our schedule because we are too busy for it.

Unbelief. We don't see how even ten minutes of pray can make a difference.

Discouragement. We have been praying and nothing is happening, and we give up.

The devil wants you to give up on prayer. He tells you, "God can't change, so why pray?" or "What's going to happen will happen anyway, so why waste your time?" What a lie from the deceiver! He takes the word of God and twists it to keep us powerless and defeated. This is what God's word says:

> "For I Am the Lord, *I do not change*; therefore you are not consumed, O sons of Jacob. Yet from the days of your fathers you have gone away from My ordinances and have not kept them. *Return to Me, and I will return to you,"* says the Lord of host. "But you say, in what way shall we return?" "Will a man rob God? Yet you have robbed Me! But you say in what way have we robbed You? In tithes and offerings *you are cursed with a curse, for you have robbed Me,* even this whole nation. Bring all the tithes into the storehouse that there may be food in My house, and try Me now in this" says the Lord of hosts, "If I will not open for you the widows of heaven and pour out for you such blessing that there will not be room enough to receive it. And I will rebuke the devourer for your sakes, so that he will not destroy the fruit of your ground, nor shall the vine fail to bear fruit for you in the field" says the Lord of hosts.
>
> Malachi 3:6-11 (NKJ)

So the Lord relented from the harm which He said He would do to His people.

> Exodus 32:14 (NKJ)

The truth is, God does not change His character, Who He is, but when people pray, He does change His mind. He is a merciful God! And He loves His children! So repent, change your ways to His ways, and return to Him, and He will return to you.

YOU CAN HEAR GOD

Hearing God is not something you do. Hearing God is who we are!

> Most assuredly, I say to you he who does not enter the sheepfold by the door, but climbs up some other way, the same is a thief and a robber. But he who enters by the door is the shepherd of the sheep. To him the door keeper opens, and the sheep hear his voice, and he calls his own sheep by name and leads them out. And when he brings out his own sheep, he goes before them, and the sheep follow him, for they know his voice.
>
> John 10:1-4 (NKJ)

We are God's children. His creation made by His hands, spoken into existence. He breathed life into us and formed us uniquely for His will, His purpose, and His good pleasure. All so that we may surrender to the King, our Savior Jesus, and draw closer to our Father. He wants to reestablish the personal relationship that was lost in the garden because of sin. Jesus was sent to reconcile us to our Father. It's all about reestablishing a personal relationship through Jesus to our Father. He wants us to draw close to Him and Him draw close to us. He wants to finish the great work He started in us when He created us. He wants to spend eternity with His children, and He sent Jesus to make that possible.

Hearing God is innate. Meaning our ability to hear God has existed in us since birth. It's a characteristic we were created with. Hearing God is also learned, by searching for it in His word and through prayer, and it's matured through use as we listen for His still small voice in our mind. He is speaking through His scriptures and guiding us in His will or purpose for us. God does speak to His children.

> For I have known him, in order that he may command his children and his household after him, that they keep the way of the Lord, to do righteousness and justice, that the Lord may bring to Abraham what He has spoken to him.
>
> Genesis 18:19 (NKJ)

The Bible is the general will of God. The specific will of God comes from asking the Holy Spirit.

> I still have many things to say to you, but you cannot bear them now.
>
> John 16:12 (NKJ)

We are His friend. His chosen people.

> For you are a holy people to the Lord your God, and the Lord has chosen you to be a people for Himself, a special treasure above all the peoples who are on the face of the earth.
>
> Deuteronomy 14:2 (NKJ)

We all, as children of God, can hear His voice and prophesy as He wills it in us through His abundant grace. Prophesying is speaking or writing by divine inspiration as the Spirit of the Lord reveals things to you.

> Then Moses said to him, "Are you zealous for my sake? Oh, that all the Lords people were prophets and that the Lord would put His Spirit upon them!"
>
> Numbers 11:29 (NKJ)

And it shall come to pass in the last days, says God, that I will pour out My Spirit on all flesh, your sons and your daughters shall prophesy, your young men shall see visions, your old men shall dream dreams. And on My menservants and on My maidservants I will pour out My Spirit in those days; and they shall prophesy. I will show wonders in heaven above and signs in the earth beneath: Blood and fire and vapor of smoke. The sun shall be turned into darkness, and the moon into blood, before the coming of the great and awesome day of the Lord. And it shall come to pass that whoever calls on the name of the Lord shall be saved.

Acts 2:17-21 (NKJ)

Pursue love, and desire spiritual gifts but especially that you may prophesy. For he who speaks in a tongue does not speak to men but to God, for no one understands him, however, in the Spirit he speaks mysteries. But he who prophesies speaks edification and exhortation and comfort to men.

1 Corinthians 14:1-3 (NKJ)

For you can all prophesy one by one, that all men may learn and all may be encouraged.

1 Corinthians 14:31 (NKJ)

What you hear or see, in prophecy, should be edifying and encouraging to those around you. It is a gift of the Spirit, and it should fall in line with Gods word and the fruits of the Spirit to build people up and encourage them in their walk with the Lord.

Value His voice. God comes to a prepared atmosphere. Set an appointment with Him. Find a special time each day to quiet yourself, praise His name, show your gratitude and thank Him for all He is and all He has done in your life, meditate on His word, read the Bible and pray, listen for His voice, and write down thoughts that come to your mind when they line up with

His word and His character. I like to set my alarm for a little earlier in the morning and tithe the first part of my day to spending time with my Father. Feeling His presence and His love and getting His direction and His instruction from His word. The funny thing is, when I started setting an appointment to come into His presence, He started waking me up with His presence even before my alarm goes on. How awesome and faithful He is to meet with us. He craves a personal relationship with us as much as we crave His presence and love. He even paid the ultimate price, His Son, in order to make a way for us to come back to Him! I'm so thankful for my Savior and my Father's love!

> You shall not need to fight in this battle, position yourselves, stand still and see the salvation of the Lord, who is with you, O Judah and Jerusalem! Do not fear or be dismayed; tomorrow go out against them, for the Lord is with you.
>
> 2 Chronicles 20:17 (NKJ)

> Be still, and know that I am God; I will be exalted among the nations, I will be exalted in the earth!
>
> Psalm 46:10 (NKJ)

> *Now in the morning*, having risen a long time before daylight, He went out and departed to a solitary place, and there He prayed.
>
> Mark 1:35 (NKJ)

> *I rise before the dawning of the morning*, and cry for help; I hope in your word. My eyes are awake through the night watches, that I may meditate on your word.
>
> Psalm 119:147-148 (NKJ)

Again, hearing God is innate. It's something that we were created to do. We were born with it, and we can build or strengthen our ability. God says,

And you will seek Me and find Me, when you search for Me with all your heart.

Jeremiah 29:13 (NKJ)

How do we hear? Through His word, by the Holy Spirit, through visions and dreams and even through angels who are His messengers.

How do we differentiate His voice from ours? You read and learn His word and meditate on it. In other words, read the owner's manual from the manufacturer to recognize the owner's voice.

So then faith comes by hearing, and hearing by the word of God.

Romans 10:17 (NKJ)

And He opened their understanding, that they might comprehend the scriptures.

Luke 24:45 (NKJ)

Christianity is not a "religion." It's a relationship with God our Father. Spend time with Him and build your relationship. Fasting also helps. Giving up worldly things that you love to participate in, like TV watching, internet surfing, movies, going shopping, and favorite foods you love to eat. Do this for a determined period of time in order to make more time to draw closer to Him and hear His direction for your life, or to get an answer to a question you have, or a prayer you want answered. Seek His voice, and the Holy Spirit will speak to your spirit.

But as for me, when they were sick, my clothing was sack cloth; I humbled myself with fasting, and my prayer would return to my own heart.

Psalm 35:13 (NKJ)

Communicate with God by praying and getting still to listen. You can even journal what you hear (the thoughts that come to your mind). Study books on "how to hear God." There are a lot of good books on the topic. Most important though is committing to obey God when He speaks!

> My sheep hear My voice, and I know them, and they follow Me.
>
> John 10:27 (NKJ)

> But He answered and said, "It is written 'Man shall not live by bread alone, but by every word that proceeds from the mouth of God.'"
>
> Matthew 4:4 (NKJ)

> So He humbled you, allowed you to hunger, and fed you with manna which you did not know nor did your fathers know, that He might make you know that man shall not live by bread alone. But man lives by every word that proceeds from the mouth of the Lord.
>
> Deuteronomy 8:3 (NKJ)

> So shall My word be that goes forth from My mouth. It shall not return to Me void, but it shall accomplish what I please, and it shall prosper in the thing for which I sent it.
>
> Isaiah 55:11 (NKJ)

God speaks to us in the way we were created to understand. There is no set way because we were all created uniquely for different purposes. He does speak in a "spirit to spirit" exchange, and He does speak the truth. The lowest level of communicating is when we ask what to do or where to go or if it's His will that we buy a house or car and so on. It is important to consult Him on these things, but the important questions are "Who am I?" and "What is Your purpose for my life?" He responds in the way we personally understand. Visual is seeing through visions or dreams. Auditory is hearing Him by words in our mind. Kinesics is in actions or impressions or urges to do something. When receiving His word, ask yourself if what you're receiving produces the fruit of the Spirit and does it line up with scripture, encouraging and setting people free.

> But the fruit of the Spirit is love, joy, peace, longsuffering, kindness, goodness, faithfulness, gentleness, self control. Against such there is no law.
>
> Galatians 5:22 (NKJ)

Learning the Bible is like learning a new language. You have to practice and meditate on it. When you learn His language, you will understand more when He speaks to you in every situation. He will speak through His written word to lead and guide and teach us His ways and His will for us and He will speak through us to others.

> All scripture is given by inspiration of God, and is profitable for doctrine, for reproof, for correction, for instruction, in righteousness, that the man of God be complete, thoroughly equipped for every good work.
>
> 2 Timothy 3:16-17 (NKJ)

> For the word of God is living and powerful, and sharper than any two-edged sword, piercing even to the division of soul and spirit, and of joints and marrow, and is a discerner of the thoughts and intents of the heart.
>
> Hebrews 4:12 (NKJ)

> In the beginning was the Word, and Word was with God, and the Word was God. He was in the beginning with God. All things were made through Him, and without Him nothing was made that was made. In Him was life and the light of men.
>
> John 1:1-4 (NKJ)

We are receivers of the Kingdom of God which is all around us. He created everything. We are to plug into the power source and invite Him in to reside in us. We are to seek first the Kingdom of God, His presence, His voice, His direction, asking what He wants and what He is saying to us. When we seek the Kingdom first in all things, it has an amazing effect on our lives. Entering it changes us (transforms us). The Sabbath is a day to rest, to still our lives and listen to God. It's for meditating on His word and getting direction for the week ahead. Honoring God by setting aside a day to receive His word and receive His direction for our lives and receive His perfect rest after a long week. He refreshes and reenergizes us. Have you been honoring the Lord's Sabbath, or are you running on fumes from lack of rest and restoration?

FAITH

As new believers, we will feel in conflict with our new belief system. On one hand, there is the world and ways of the world we were raised up in and see before our eyes as truth. Things we have believed to be true through our life experiences. On the other hand, there is God's way, which is spelled out in the Bible. The conflict comes in when we try to establish the "new truth" in our lives. So let's talk about faith.

> So then faith comes by hearing, and hearing by the word of God.
>
> Romans 10:17 (NKJ)

First off, you have to read the word of God to know the word of God. As you read, you will discover what God says is the truth. Faith is not believing for something. Faith is believing in some One.

> Now faith is the substance of things hoped for, the evidence of things not seen. For by it the elders obtained a good testimony. By faith we understand that the worlds were framed by the word of God, So that the things which are seen were not made of things which are visible.
>
> Hebrews 11:1-3 (NKJ)

Jesus is the substance, what we put our hope in. The word of God is the evidence.

> But without faith it is impossible to please Him, for he who comes to God must believe that He is and that He is a rewarder of those who diligently seek Him.
>
> Hebrews 11:6 (NKJ)

Even though we can't see God, we believe He created the earth we live in and everything in the heavens and on earth. Even though we can't see Jesus, we believe He was born and walked the earth and died for our sins on the cross and rose again and ascended into heaven to sit at the right hand of God. It takes faith in things unseen to receive salvation.

> But what does it say? "The word is near you, in your mouth and in your heart" (that is, the word of faith which we preach); that if you confess with your mouth the Lord Jesus and believe in your heart that God has raised Him from the dead, you will be saved. For with the heart one believes unto righteousness, and with the mouth confession is made unto salvation.
>
> Romans 10:8-10 (NKJ)

The Bible was written by many people but there is only one Author. When we believe in our hearts that every word written in the Bible is the truth, our faith in the word will grow.

> All scripture is given by inspiration of God, and is profitable for doctrine, for reproof, for correction, for instruction in righteousness, that a man of God be complete, thoroughly equipped for every good work.
>
> 2 Timothy 3:16 (NKJ)

> For the word of God is living and powerful, and sharper than any two-edged sword, piercing even to the division of

soul and spirit, and of joints and marrow, and is a discerner of the thoughts and intents of the heart.

Hebrews 4:12 (NKJ)

The spoken word is living and powerful. As we learn and understand the word of God, our belief or faith grows. We can start speaking the promises, and spoken facts, found in the Bible into our lives and the lives of others through prayer. Then get ready to see miracles happen, because as it says above, "The word of God is living and powerful."

So shall My word be that goes forth from My mouth; It shall not return to Me void, but it shall accomplish what I please, and it shall prosper in the thing for which I sent it.

Isaiah 55:11 (NKJ)

Oh, how I love Your law! It is my meditation all the day. You, through Your commandments, make me wiser than my enemies; for they are ever with me. I have more understanding than all my teachers, for Your testimonies are my meditation.

Psalm 119:97-99 (NKJ)

Let the word of God dwell in you richly in all wisdom, teaching and admonishing one another in psalms and hymns and spiritual songs, singing with grace in your hearts to the Lord.

Colossians 3:16 (NKJ)

Ask, and it will be given to you; seek, and you will find; knock, and it will be opened to you.

Matthew 7:7 (NKJ)

Therefore I say to you, whatever things you ask when you pray, believe that you receive them, and you will have them.

Matthew 11:24 (NKJ)

As you are praying in faith for an answered prayer, remember God's timing is not the same as our timing when it comes to responses. Also remember, people are not our source when it comes to receiving answered prayers, God is our source. God knows we need it already, and our need does not move God, but faith does move God. We must seek first the Kingdom of God and His way of doing things to see results. The Kingdom of God system lines up with His word where King Jesus makes decrees full of life, health, and freedom, and the Bible is the constitution of the Kingdom.

> Therefore do not worry, saying "What shall we eat? Or what shall we drink? Or what shall we wear?" For after all these things the Gentiles seek. For your heavenly Father knows that you need all these things. But seek first the kingdom of God and His righteousness, and all these things shall be added to you.
>
> Matthew 6:31-33 (NKJ)

Faith in God's word is having confidence in God's word, saying, "I'm taking a stand. I'm not moving, regardless of what I feel or what I see."

> Therefore do not cast away your confidence, which has great reward. For you have need of endurance, so that after you have done the will of God, you may receive the promise.
>
> Hebrews 10:35-36 (NKJ)

Patience is endurance. It's being constantly the same, not changing what you know is the truth. The devil will attack your confidence with doubt and fear to get you off track. But you are not healed because of the way you feel, you are healed because Jesus said so. You are prosperous or wealthy because the word of God says so and not because of what you see or experience. You have need of patience to see the results of your faith. The issue is not the ability of the word. The issue is our confidence in the word. When we follow the will of God, He adds all things we need to accomplish His will and purpose in our lives. We don't have to know the details of how God is going to do it or be able to see how God's going to do it, or even have a total understanding of how God's going to do it. All we have to do is believe He will because the word says it. God operates in faith. But if you don't read the Bible, how will you know what has already been done for you? How will you know what His truth is so you can speak it into your life?

> My people are destroyed for lack of knowledge. Because you have rejected knowledge, I also will reject you from being priest for Me; because you have forgotten the law of your God, I also will forget your children.
>
> Hosea 4:6 (NKJ)

> Preach the word! Be ready in season and out of season. Convince, rebuke, exhort, with all longsuffering and teaching. For the time will come when they will not endure sound doctrine, but according to their own desires, because they have itching ears, they will heap up for themselves teachers; and they will turn their ears away from the truth, and be turned aside to fables. But you be watchful in all things, endure afflictions, do the work of an evangelist, fulfill your ministry.
>
> 2 Timothy 4:2-5 (NKJ)

> And they overcame him by the blood of the Lamb and by the word of their testimony, and they did not love their lives to the death.
>
> Revelation 12:11 (NKJ)

How will we stand, in these last days, for our Savior Jesus? If you don't know the word, you will be defeated by your lack of knowledge. As Revelation says, they overcame him (the devil) by the blood of the Lamb and by the word of their testimony (truths spoken in the Bible).

Spiritual Growth and Enlightenment through Scripture

Therefore, leaving the discussion of the elementary principles of Christ, let us go on to perfection, not laying again the foundation of repentance from dead works and of faith toward God, of the doctrine of baptisms, of laying on of hands, of resurrection of the dead, and of eternal judgment. And this we will do if God permits.

Hebrews 6:1-3 (NKJ)

SPIRITUAL GROWTH

Therefore, leaving the discussion of the elementary principles of Christ, let us go on to perfection, not laying again the foundation of repentance from dead works and of faith toward God, of the doctrine of baptisms, of laying on of hands, of resurrection of the dead, and of eternal judgment. And this we will do if God permits. For it is impossible for those who were once enlightened, and have tasted the heavenly gift, and have become partakers of the Holy Spirit, and have tasted the good word of God and the powers of the age to come, if they fall away, to renew them again to repentance, since they crucify again for themselves the Son of God, and put Him to an open shame. For the earth which drinks in the rain that often comes upon it, and bears herbs useful for those by whom it is cultivated, receives blessing from God; but if it bears thorns and briers, it is rejected and near to being cursed, whose end is to be burned.

Hebrews 6:1-8 (NKJ)

READING AND MEDITATING on the word of God brings about spiritual growth. As you continue to read and meditate on the word of God each day, understanding the basic truths about faith, baptism, healing, resurrection of the dead, judgment of Christ, praying, repentance, and so forth, God will increase your understanding as He wills it to be so. He wants us to be transformed from our worldly or fleshly way of thinking to a Kingdom of God way of thinking, and that is accomplished by reading the word of God.

> I beseech you therefore, brethren, by the mercies of God that you present your bodies a living sacrifice, holy acceptable to God, which is your reasonable service. And do not be conformed to this world, but be transformed by the renewing of your mind, that you may prove what is that good and acceptable and perfect will of God.
>
> Romans 12:1-2 (NKJ)

Part of our transformation is coming to an understanding of who we are after we accept Jesus as our Savior.

> Therefore, if anyone is in Christ, he is a new creation; old things have passed away; behold, all things have become new.
>
> 2 Corinthians 5:17 (NKJ)

We don't actually change ourselves. He changes us. We surrender our will to God. Our will is actually our mechanism for making decisions. By surrendering our will to the Lordship of Jesus, we are recognizing Him as our source of all things. We are letting go of the steering wheel and allowing Him to direct our lives. We seek to hear God's voice, and He empowers us to do His will in our lives. But again, we need to read His word to hear His word as He speaks to us. When we receive Jesus, He resides in us. When you step into His family, He gives you Him, not part of Him. He wants us to see more the way He sees, and this takes time to reprogram us into a new way of knowing. You can expect to stumble a few times because it's learning how to walk a new way. My pastor at Gateway Church in Southlake, Texas, Pastor

Robert Morris, explained this in the simplest way I have ever heard (as explained in the steps below). You can measure your spiritual growth by looking at Jesus's explanation of the parable of the sower.

> The sower sows the word. And these are the ones by the wayside where the word is sown. When they hear, satan comes immediately and takes away the word that was sown in their hearts. These likewise are the ones sown on stony ground who, when they hear the word, immediately receive it with gladness; and they have no root in themselves, and so endure only for a time. Afterward, when tribulation or persecution arises for the words sake, immediately they stumble. Now these are the ones sown among thorns; they are the ones who hear the word, and the cares of this world, the deceitfulness of riches, and the desires for other things entering in choke the word, and it becomes unfruitful. But these are the ones sown on good ground, those who hear the word, accept it, and bear fruit; some thirty fold, some sixty, and some a hundred.
>
> Mark 4:14-20 (NKJ)

Levels of change represented in the parable of the sower:
Four types of listeners are represented here:

1.   EG = Exploring God (The Fellowship Stage)

For whatever reason, they are attending church. Or asking questions about Jesus and God and heaven. But they have not believed and accepted Jesus yet. They are still seeking.

2.   BG = Beginning with God (The Relationship Stage)

These are new believers. They are learning the basics and attending church on Sunday and sometimes Wednesday and are starting to read the Bible and learn more.

3.   CG = Close to God (The Discipleship Stage)

These are hungry believers. They are eager to learn more about the Bible and more history. They are attending classes and have structured study time. "He walks with me."

4. GC = God Centered (The Lordship Stage)

These believers are going the extra step of voluntarily spending in-depth time (reading at home, meditating on the word of God). They start to walk out what they have learned by reaching out to others, giving to those in need and sharing the gospel. "I walk with Him."

Giving something of ourselves causes a move or progression in spiritual growth. What causes each move? *Giving!*

Step 1 = Giving of Self. The Truth of Grace

We believe in Jesus and give ourselves to Him and receive the gift of grace which is salvation. Just believing and receiving God's gift (EG to BG)

Step 2 = Giving of Time. Time in Gods Word (Bible)

Believing and following His word, spending time reading the Bible, praying, and simply building a relationship with Him (BG to CG)

Step 3 = Giving of Control. Total Love, Total Faith, Total Surrender to Him

When you would lay your life down for Him and follow His will for you. Walking out your role as an ambassador for God's Kingdom (CG to GC)

When seeking salvation for people you know, remember Satan comes immediately to take the word from their heart. We should follow up to keep giving the word back. These are some of the things they need to hear:

1. Salvation is not based on works. It's based on faith (belief), and it's a free gift.

> For by grace you have been saved through faith, and that not of yourself; it is the gift of God.
>
> Ephesians 2:8 (NKJ)

2. It's a free gift: Jesus paid it all—we owe nothing—it's free.

> For the wages of sin is death, but the gift of God is eternal life in Christ Jesus our Lord.
>
> Romans 6:23 (NKJ)

3. It's easy to receive: It's just believing and confessing our belief in the life, death, and resurrection of Jesus.

> That if you confess with your mouth the Lord Jesus and believe in your heart that God has raised Him from the dead, you will be saved. For with the heart one believes unto righteousness and with the mouth confession is made unto salvation.
>
> Romans 10:9 (NKJ)

Satan's plan is to keep us out of the word. In scripture, there are many different terms that are used to describe Satan, demons, and evil spirits, such as birds—beasts—scorpions—serpents—demons—evil spirits—fallen angels.

God's plan is to hide the word in our hearts. If we memorize the word through meditation on the word, then Satan can't take it from us.

> Your word I have hidden in my heart that I might not sin against You.
>
> Psalm 119:11 (NKJ)

> I will meditate on Your precepts, and contemplate Your ways.
>
> Psalm 119:15 (NKJ)

> But if you don't drive out the inhabitants of the land from before you, then it shall be that those whom you let remain shall be irritants in your eyes and thorns in your sides, and they shall harass you in the land where you dwell.
>
> Numbers 33:55 (NKJ)

Some of the things that distract us from hearing and receiving the word of God are as follows:

1. Cares of this world: too many tasks planned, don't make time to read God's word, distractions while reading.

2. Deceitfulness of riches: working long hours to support living outside our normal means of God's provision, covetousness.

3. Desires for other things: desiring an abundance of earthly things, keeping up a standard or appearance based on others thoughts of us.

When you get so bogged down in worldly things that you have no time for God, it's probably time for some temple cleaning. Look at how Jesus did it when He came into the temple, and there was so much going on that the temple wasn't even being used for its intended purpose anymore.

> So they came to Jerusalem. Then Jesus went into the temple and began to drive out those who bought and sold in the temple, and overturned the tables of the money changers and the seats of those who sold doves. And He would not allow anyone to carry wares through the temple. Then He taught, saying to them, "Is it not written, "My house shall be called a house of prayer for all nations?" But you have made it a den of thieves."
>
> Mark 11:15-17 (NKJ)

When we fill our lives with so many distractions and activities that we don't have time to pray and read and thank God for all He's done, then we really need to take a closer look at how we are stewarding our time each day and reprioritize what we are involved in. How do you expect to grow spiritually if you don't make time to?

Do you not know that you are the temple of God and that the Spirit of God dwells in you?

1 Corinthians 3:16 (NKJ)

PROGRESSION IN SPIRITUAL GROWTH

I dedicate part of my time each day to reading the word. The more I read, the more I progress in my spiritual growth, and I love the word so it's easy. I've heard it explained this way:

Our bodies were initially made from the dust of the earth, and we are fed with things from the earth, and when we die, our flesh returns to the earth and back to dust.

Our spirit was breathed into us from God, it's fed by the word of God, and it returns to God to receive our final destination, either heaven or hell based on our acceptance of, and surrender to, Jesus Christ, or not.

So just as our body suffers when we fail to provide food as nourishment, our spirit also suffers from lack of the word of God to nurture and bring about spiritual growth.

> For though by this time you ought to be teachers, you need someone to teach you again the first principles of the oracles of God; and you have come to need milk and not solid food. For everyone who partakes only of milk is unskilled in the word of righteousness, for he is a babe. But solid food belongs to those who are of full age, that is, those who by reason of use have their senses exercised to discern both good and evil.
>
> Hebrews 5:12-14 (NKJ)

> Therefore, leaving the discussion of the elementary principles of Christ, let us go on to perfection, not laying again the foundation of repentance from dead works and of faith toward God, of the doctrine of baptisms, of laying on of

hands, of resurrection of the dead, and of eternal judgment. And this we will do if God permits.

Hebrews 6:1-3 (NKJ)

Therefore, laying aside all malice, all deceit, hypocrisy, envy, and all evil speaking, as newborn babes, desire the pure milk of the word, that you may grow thereby.

1 Peter 2:1-2 (NKJ)

But these are the ones sown on good ground, *those who hear the word, accept it, and bear fruit*, some thirtyfold, some sixty, and some a hundred.

Mark 4:20 (NKJ)

Then He said to them, "Take heed what you hear. With the same measure you use, it will be measured to you; *and to you who hear, more will be given.* For whoever has, to him more will be given; but whoever does not have, even what he has will be taken away from him."

Mark 4:24-25 (NKJ)

So let's cover some of the basics:

- Law vs Grace
- Ten Commandments vs Love
- Faith/Grace vs works
- Repentance from Dead Works
- Doctrine of Baptisms
- Laying on of Hands and Healing
- Resurrection of the Dead
- Eternal Judgment: Heaven vs Hell and Life vs Death

LAW VS GRACE

The law is actually a measure. It helps us understand the right way to behave. It also helps us measure our progress or growth (transformation). It isn't to judge others. God's laws are the ten commandments. This law is a test that God does not grade for believers. If you miss one of them, you miss them all (fail). The law actually shows us how desperately we need a Savior. In the Old Testament, blood sacrifices were made to cover the sins committed by breaking a commandment. But just as it says, it covered but did not remove the sin. Jesus came to take all our sins in the past, present, and future upon Himself, and our part is surrendering our life to Him. Salvation (eternal life) is a free gift of God, paid in full by Jesus. He washes our sins away.

> For whoever shall keep the whole law and yet stumble in one point, he is guilty of all.
>
> James 2:10 (NKJ)

You have actually been taking this test since you were born. But for believers, Jesus took the test for us. And we have His grade through the Grace of God. Thank you, Jesus!!!

> For the grace of God that brings salvation has appeared to all men, teaching us that, denying ungodliness and worldly lusts, we should live soberly, righteously, and godly in the present age, looking for the blessed hope and glorious appearing of our great God and Savior Jesus Christ, who gave Himself for us, that He might redeem us from every lawless deed, and purify for Himself His own special people, zealous for good works. Speak these things, exhort, and rebuke with all authority. Let no one despise you.
>
> Titus 2:11-15 (NKJ)

> But before faith came, we were kept under guard by the law, kept for faith which would afterward be revealed.

Therefore law was our tutor to bring us to Christ, that we may be justified by faith. But after faith has come, we are no longer under a tutor.

Galatians 3:23-25 (NKJ)

The law is in place to tutor us until we are saved by the Grace of God and are no longer under the law, but follow the law willingly because of our faith in the word of God. The big picture is not a "right or wrong decision," but it is a "life or death decision." After you are saved, the new law is a mirror of God's word. When we look at ourselves, we should see a reflection of Jesus in us (being for what He's for). The new law reflects the parameters of God's desire for us, but it does not reflect the parameters of God's love (which has no boundaries). The new law is a map we are to follow (the will of God and the example of Jesus).

Your word is a lamp to my feet and a light to my path.

Psalm 119:105 (NKJ)

TEN COMMANDMENTS

This is a list of the ten commandments found in Exodus 20:1-17 that God spoke to Moses saying, "I AM the Lord your God, who brought you out of the land of Egypt, out of the house of bondage."

1. You shall have no other gods before Me.

2. You shall not make for yourself a carved image—any likeness of anything that is in heaven above, or that is in the earth beneath, or that is in the water underneath the earth, you shall not bow down to them nor serve them. For I, the Lord your God, Am a jealous God, visiting the iniquity of the fathers upon the children to the third and fourth generations of those who hate Me, but show-

ing mercy to thousands, to those who love Me and keep My commandments.

3. You shall not take the name of the Lord your God in vain, for the Lord will not hold him guiltless who takes His name in vain.

4. Remember the Sabbath day, to keep it holy. Six days you shall labor and do all your work, but the seventh day is the Sabbath of the Lord your God. In it you shall do no work, nor your son, nor your daughter, nor your male or female servant, nor your cattle, nor your stranger who is within your gates. For in six days the Lord made the heavens and the earth, the sea, and all that is in them, and rested on the seventh day. Therefore the Lord blessed the Sabbath day and hallowed it.

***The first four commandments are our relationship with God.

5. Honor your father and your mother, that your days may be long upon the land which the Lord your God is giving you.

6. You shall not murder.

7. You shall not commit adultery.

8. You shall not steal.

9. You shall not bear false witness against your neighbor.

10. You shall not covet your neighbors' house, wife, male servant, female servant, ox, donkey, nor anything that is your neighbors.

***The last six commandments are our relationship with others.

We truly need to stop trying to justify what we are doing. If it's wrong, then it's wrong, so just repent or change your ways and come clean with God. If you surrender your problems to Him, He is faithful to forgive. The commandments actually show us our need for a Savior and the Grace of God. God wants us to be totally committed to Him, for Him, and on Him, not on worldly possessions. Grace of God deals with the heart. The power of His grace is what changes us. Christianity deals with relationships, how we treat each other. We are to love God and love others. Jesus is the only way to get to heaven. We can't be good enough to get there on our own. Before the crucifixion of Jesus, He was speaking with His disciples and shared a new commandment with them. The new commandment is a "key" to following the original "ten commandments" given by God to Moses. Jesus said,

> A new commandment I give to you, that you love one another; as I have loved you, that you also love one another. By this all will know that you are My disciples. If you have love for one another.
>
> John 13:34-35 (NKJ)

> If you keep My commandments, you will abide in My love, just as I have kept My Fathers commandments and abide in His love.
>
> John 15:10 (NKJ)

> You did not choose Me, but I chose you and appointed you that you should go and bear fruit, and that fruit should remain, that whatever you ask the Father in My name He may give you. "These things I command you, that you love one another."
>
> John 15:16-17 (NKJ)

If we love each other the way Jesus loved us and put God first in all we do, then how can we not follow God's commandments? If you love through the Father's love and with our Savior's love, none of the commandments will be broken.

> For all the law is fulfilled in one word, even in this "You shall love your neighbor as yourself".
>
> Galatians 5:14 (NKJ)

Love suffers long and is kind; love does not envy; love does not parade itself, is not puffed up; does not behave rudely, does not seek its own, is not provoked, thinks no evil; does not rejoice in iniquity, but rejoices in the truth; bears all things, believes all things, hopes all things, endures all things. Love never fails.

1 Corinthians 13:4-7 (NKJ)

FAITH AND GRACE VS WORKS AND DEAD WORKS

What is righteousness? It's being in right standing with God. Our righteousness does not depend on our performance or deeds. It depends on our right standing with God. I get to go to heaven because of the blood of Jesus and by the Grace of God. By faith or belief in what Jesus accomplished on the cross for us thousands of years ago. Not by any work I could ever do on this earth.

Jesus said, "This is the work of God, that you believe in Him whom He sent."

John 6:29 (NKJ)

All we have to do is believe in Jesus and surrender to Him by speaking our belief out loud. Ask Him to come into your life and be your Savior—that's it!!!

Now faith is the substance of things hoped for, the evidence of things not seen.

Hebrews 11:1 (NKJ)

That if you confess with your mouth the Lord Jesus and believe in your heart that God has raised Him from the dead, you will be saved.

Romans 10:9 (NKJ)

> For by grace you have been saved through faith and that not of yourselves; it is the gift of God. Not of works, lest anyone should boast. For we are His workmanship, created in Christ Jesus for good works, which God prepared before hand that we should walk in them.
>
> Ephesians 2:8-10 (NKJ)

A dead work is something not initiated by God or by hearing God. It's something we do to try to gain God's approval. We are not saved by works but by the grace of God, which is a free gift. The old covenant was based on the law and following the ten commandments. The law was put in place to tutor us until we are saved by grace and are no longer under the law, but choose to follow the law willingly because of our faith in the word of God. The new covenant is through Jesus and is simply loving God and each other. We learn God's word and become more like Jesus, being for what God is for. The new covenant of law reflects the parameters of God's desire for us through His word but does not reflect the parameters of God's love (which has no boundaries). God said,

> Of every tree of the garden you may freely eat; but of the tree of knowledge of good and evil you shall not eat, for in the day that you eat of it, you shall surely die.
>
> Genesis 2:16-17 (NKJ)

The tree of knowledge represented: the law/right vs wrong/good vs evil. Man was deceived into thinking if they ate from the tree of knowledge, they could be more like God, but they were already made in His image and were in right standing with God, with the ability to be in His presence and talk with Him. The tree of life represented the grace of God and His understanding: Life/Jesus/connected through the Spirit. Eating from the tree of knowledge brought spiritual separation from God (because of sin/disobedience).

It's only by the grace of God (free gift that can't be earned) and faith (our belief) in Jesus Christ that we can be reconnected with the Spirit of God and hear Him speak into our lives again as He brings understanding through His word.

> But before faith came, we were kept under guard by the law, kept for faith which would afterward be revealed. Therefore the law was our tutor to bring us to Christ, that we may be justified by faith. But after faith has come, we are no longer under a tutor.
>
> Galatians 3:23-25 (NKJ)

So the law is in place to tutor us until we are saved by grace, and we are no longer under the law, but follow the law willingly, because of our faith in the word of God and our love for Him and each other.

> Jesus said, "Do not think that I come to destroy the law or the prophets. I did not come to destroy but to fulfill. For assuredly, I say to you, till heaven and earth pass away, one jot or one tittle will by no means pass from the law till all is fulfilled. Whoever therefore breaks one of the least of these commandments, and teaches men so, shall be called least in the kingdom of heaven; but whoever does and teaches them, he shall be called great in the kingdom of heaven. For I say to you, that unless your righteousness exceeds the righteousness of the scribes and Pharisees, you will by no means enter the kingdom of heaven.
>
> Matthew 5:17-19 (NKJ)

There are basically three different ways we can see ourselves, and the view we have of our self determines how we interact with people around us:

1. An Orphan—as fatherless, when we feel we need approval from people around us and we don't feel like we belong,

and it's hard to really commit to anything mostly out of fear of failure.

2. As a Slave—we work really hard to gain acceptance, our position depends on our performance, we feel like we have to earn approval, we concentrate on our behavior, it's all about "look at me," the need to be seen or recognized.

3. As a Son—having faith in what the word of God says about who He says we are.

> For you are all sons of God through faith in Christ Jesus. For as many of you as were baptized into Christ have put on Christ. There is neither Jew nor Greek, there is neither slave nor free, there is neither male nor female; for you are all one in Christ Jesus. And if you are Christ's, then you are Abraham's seed, and heirs according to the promise.
>
> Galatians 3:26-29 (NKJ)

> But when the fullness of the time had come, God sent forth His Son, born of a woman, born under the law, to redeem those who were under the law, that we might receive the adoption as sons. And because you are sons, God has sent forth the Spirit of His Son into your hearts, crying out "Abba Father!" Therefore you are no longer a slave but a son, and if a son, then an heir of God through Christ.
>
> Galatians 4:4-7 (NKJ)

Grace = God's part (it's for us but independent of us)

It's not earned and not deserved. It's a free gift from a loving Father.

Faith = Our part (which is receiving a gift of God). It's our response to what God offers. We reach out and receive His promises by faith (belief) in His word. The things, which are provided by God's grace, we must first believe and receive them by our faith or belief or trust in Him. But faith without works is dead.

Just believing God or hearing God is not enough. You must act on what you believe or hear.

Works = putting our faith into action:

> What does it profit, my brethren, if someone says he has faith but does not have works? Can faith save him? If a brother or sister is naked and destitute of daily food, and one of you says to them "Depart in peace, be warmed and filled," but you do not give them the things which are needed for the body, what does it profit them? Thus also faith by itself, if it does not have works, is dead. But someone will say "You have faith, and I have works" show me your faith without your works, and I will show you my faith by my works. You believe that there is one God. You do well. Even the demons believe and tremble! But do you want to know, O foolish man, that faith without works is dead? Was not Abraham our father justified by works when he offered Isaac his son on the altar? Do you see that faith was working together with his works, and by works his faith was made perfect? And the scripture was fulfilled which said, "Abraham believed God, and it was accounted to him for righteousness" and he was called the friend of God. You see then that a man is justified by works, and not by faith alone. Likewise was not Rahab the harlot also justified by works when she received the messengers and sent them out another way? For as the body without the spirit is dead, so faith without works is dead also.
>
> James 2:14-26 (NKJ)

It's not enough just to believe or have faith that Jesus died for our sins and rose again. We have to act on our faith and confess it with our mouths. It's not enough just to hear God tell us to do something and believe Him, but we also have to act on what He tells us to do.

Dead Works = Actions which have no benefit to the kingdom of heaven.

Do not lay up for yourself treasures on earth, where moth and rust destroy and where thieves break in and steal; but lay up for yourselves treasures in heaven, where neither moth nor rust destroys and where thieves do not break in and steal. "For where your treasure is, there your heart will also be."

Matthew 6:19-21 (NKJ)

What is always on your mind? People were always on Jesus's mind just as people are on the Father's mind. People last forever and we are His treasure. It's the whole reason Jesus came to this earth. So what kind of stuff takes up your time? Work, exercise, TV, movies, house cleaning, errands, ball games, hair appointments, dance recitals, dinner parties, vacations, etc. The list could be endlessly full of various activities that take up all our free time. And none of these are bad in and of themselves, but where does the kingdom of heaven fit into all of this? If you concentrate entirely on worldly things and don't make time to concentrate on God's work, "saving people," you will miss your purpose by holding on too tightly to worldly things (dead works).

Do you not know that you are the temple of God and that the Spirit of God dwells in you?

1 Corinthians 3:16 (NKJ)

So they came to Jerusalem. Then Jesus went into the temple and began to drive out those who bought and sold in the temple, and overturned the tables of the money changers and the seats of those who sold doves. And He would not allow anyone to carry wares through the temple. Then He taught, saying to them, "Is it not written, "My house shall be called a house of prayer for all nations? But you have made it a den of thieves." And the scribes and chief priests heard it and sought how they might destroy Him; for they feared Him, because all the people were astonished at His teaching.

Mark 11:15-18 (NKJ)

From that time Jesus began to preach and to say, "Repent, for the kingdom of heaven is at hand."

Matthew 4:17 (NKJ)

Repenting of Dead Works starts with recognizing things that are of no benefit to the kingdom and agreeing to change our ways to line up with His will. Are we filling up our lives with so much stuff that we are not taking time to read His word, worship Him, and thank Him each day for all He provides? If so, then it's time to repent and change your ways. Is it time to flip the temple tables and make room for our King? The One who holds the keys to our future and now!

REPENTING OF DEAD WORKS— PRAYER OF CONFESSION

1. Admit your sin as the Holy Spirit puts it on your heart that you have done something against Gods will, and ask to be washed clean.

2. If you slip up and do the same things again, confess it again and ask Father to help you change your ways. Don't stop confessing just because you think God's tired of hearing you repent from it. God wants us to surrender all, especially the hard stuff because nothing is too big or too small for the Creator of the Universe!

But Jesus looked at them and said, "With men it is impossible, but not with God; for with God all things are possible.

Mark 10:27 (NKJ)

But Jesus said to him, "If you can believe, all things are possible to him who believes."

Mark 9:23 (NKJ)

But He said, "The things which are impossible with men are possible with God."

Luke 18:27 (NKJ)

If you stop confessing your sin, you start accepting the sin as "just the way it is."

If we confess our sins, He is faithful and just to forgive us our sins and to cleanse us from all unrighteousness.

1 John 1:9 (NKJ)

Important things to remember:

1. Don't try to justify your sin with excuses: I was scared, I was angry, I was worrying, stressing, etc. Sin is a form of spiritual adultery because you are actually yielding to something other than God. Stop justifying, and just admit that you did it. You sinned against God, and agree with God that it was a sin.

   So it came to pass, through her casual harlotry, that she defiled the land and committed adultery with stones and trees.

   Jeremiah 3:9 (NKJ)

(which are altars to worship other gods and carved idols). Is there anything you are putting before God in importance?

2. Ask God to forgive you, to wash you clean, and to renew you. God does forgive us when we ask. When you stop asking for forgiveness and hold onto things instead of surrendering them to God, then you get further from God. Get rid of the barriers, confess, repent, and draw closer to Him. He is waiting with open arms!

   "Yet from the days of your fathers you have gone away from My ordinances and have not kept them. Return to Me, and I will return to you." Says the Lord of hosts.

   Malachi 3:7 (NKJ)

GOD is our refuge and strength, a very present help in trouble.

Psalm 46:1 (NKJ)

Until now you have asked nothing in My name. Ask, and you will receive, that your joy may be full.

John 16:24 (NKJ)

3. Accept the Father's forgiveness and thank Him. You don't have to walk around sad about it for a while. Jesus totally paid the price for our sins, past, present, and future, so just accept it for "It is finished!"

    But this Man (Jesus), after He had offered one sacrifice for sins forever, sat down at the right hand of God.

    Hebrews 10:21 (NKJ)

    Then He adds, "Their sins and their lawless deeds I will remember no more."

    Hebrews 10:17 (NKJ)

    If we confess our sins, He is faithful and just to forgive us our sins and to cleanse us from all unrighteousness.

    1 John 1:9 (NKJ)

This is a parable that was spoken by Jesus in the book of Matthew which had a great impact on my life when I meditated on its meaning. The understanding of the great love He has for us just intensified as I read it and it fed my spirit.

"Again, *the kingdom of heaven* is like *treasure* hidden in *a field*, which *a man* found and *hid*; and *for joy over it* he goes and *sells all that he has* and *buys that field*."

Matthew 13:44 (NKJ)

The *kingdom of heaven* is "all" the believers. We are citizens of heaven.

The *field* represents the world.

Jesus sees us as *His treasure*.

And of course, *the man* is Jesus.

Jesus willingly gave His life to pay the price of sin for all! All we have to do is accept Him as our Savior. "Surrender"

> For you were bought at a price, therefore glorify God in your body and in your spirit, which are Gods.
>
> 1 Corinthians 6:20 (NKJ)

Jesus came to earth, found us (His treasure), and hid us in Himself.

> For you died, and your life is hidden with Christ in God.
>
> Colossians 3:3 (NKJ)

> Now therefore, if you will indeed obey My voice and keep My covenant, then you shall be a special treasure to Me above all people, for all the earth is Mine.
>
> Exodus 19:5 (NKJ)

Jesus paid the ultimate price, His life. He shed His precious blood for us because He loves us that much!

DOCTRINE OF BAPTISMS

There are three baptisms. Blood, Water, and Spirit. The *first baptism* is when the Holy Spirit quickens our understanding of Jesus our Savior. Then believing in our heart that Jesus is real and died for us on the cross (shedding His blood as a sacrifice for our sins) and rose again from the grave. We confess our beliefs out loud and ask Him to come into our lives as our Savior. Salvation is the first step, by the blood Jesus shed for us.

For by one Spirit we were baptized into one body –
whether Jew or Greeks, whether slaves or free – and have
all been made to drink into one Spirit.

1 Corinthians 12:13 (NKJ)

But God demonstrates His own love toward us, in that
while we were still sinners, Christ died for us. Much more
then, having now been justified by His blood, we shall be
saved from wrath through Him. For if when we were enemies we were reconciled to God through the death of His
Son, much more, having been reconciled, we shall be saved
by His life. And not only that, but we also rejoice in God
through our Lord Jesus Christ, through whom we have
now received the reconciliation.

Romans 5:8-11 (NKJ)

The *second baptism* is when the disciples baptize you in water,
which is a proclamation of dying to your old self and rising again
a new man to walk in the ways of Jesus. Just as Jesus died and was
buried and arose again, going under the water represents a burial
with Christ and rising out of the water is being raised up to walk
a new life with Jesus.

Go therefore and make disciples of all the nations, baptizing them in the name of the Father and of the Son, and of
the Holy Spirit.

Matthew 28:19 (NKJ)

I did not know Him, but He who sent me to baptize with
water said to me, "Upon whom you see the Spirit descend-
ing and remaining on Him, this is He who baptizes with
the Holy Spirit.

John 1:33 (NKJ)

I indeed baptize you with water unto repentance, but He
who is coming after me is mightier than I, whose sandals I

am not worthy to carry. He will baptize you with the Holy Spirit and fire.

> Matthew 3:11 (NKJ)

The *third baptism* is when Jesus baptizes us in the Holy Spirit. When filled with the Holy Spirit, we have the power to walk in the newness as a new or transforming man. The power to change is given by Jesus by Him filling us with the Holy Spirit.

> I indeed baptize you with water, but He will baptize you with the Holy Spirit.
>
> Mark 1:8 (NKJ)

> John answered, saying to all "I indeed baptize you with water; but One mightier than I is coming, whose sandal strap I am not worthy to loose. He will baptize you with the Holy Spirit and fire.
>
> Luke 3:16 (NKJ)

You also can see the three types of baptisms in 1 John.

> And there are three that bear witness on earth: the Spirit, the water, and the blood; and these three agree as one.
>
> 1 John 5:8 (NKJ)

Blood = Salvation = Receiving Jesus as our Savior.
Water = baptism in water (submersion) dying to old self.
Spirit = Jesus gives us or fills us with the Holy Spirit, so we receive the power to walk in the new life. The Holy Spirit enables us to do the will of God.

> Then Peter said, "Repent and let every one of you be baptized in the name of Jesus Christ for the remission of sins; and you shall receive the gift of the Holy Spirit. For the promise is to you and to your children, and to all who are afar off, as many as the Lord our God will call.
>
> Acts 2:38-39 (NKJ)

How it all fits together:

The Holy Spirit draws us to Jesus, Jesus reconnects us to Father, Father gives us Jesus, and Jesus gives us the Holy Spirit. Is there anything more complete than that? It is a divinely finished work!

LAYING ON OF HANDS AND HEALING

The Bible is full of accounts of miraculous healing, but many people think that healing is "an impossibility" in this day and time. That is surely something the devil would like us to believe. Lots of people have the notion that the record of miraculous healings we read about in the Bible are historical events or maybe parables or not applicable to our lives today. Some believe healing miracles were specific to the disciples of Jesus or the first twelve who walked with Jesus and they are all dead so they can't happen in this day and age. But what if we have faith in the Bible and God's ability? Is our lack of faith hindering our experiencing this supernatural outpouring that He is still capable of doing today? Has God changed His abilities? I think not! People, God can do anything that is in His will to perform! He can work through anyone He chooses to work through, and He can heal all by Himself. His ways and thoughts are much higher than ours. This is not to say He doesn't heal through doctors. He most certainly does, all the time. We have lots of gifted doctors. But when we get a bad report from the doctor, we should not automatically look at it as a death sentence; we should look at it as an opportunity to call on God to accomplish something that is impossible for us to do on our own. A chance to give Him praise and build a testimony to share with others.

God does not want us walking around sick and diseased. If He did, He would not have sent His Son to suffer for us, stating that, "by His stripes, we are healed." This does not mean we won't face adversities in life, but that with each struggle, God will bear us up and allow us to endure the tough times as we walk in faith, until His promise is made manifest in our lives. God has the cure for any sickness the enemy tries to afflict us with. He is the Great Physician!

> But those who wait on the Lord shall renew their strength; they shall mount up with wings like eagles, they shall run and not be weary, they shall walk and not faint.
>
> Isaiah 40:31 (NKJ)

> And shall God not avenge His own elect who cry out day and night to Him, though He bears long with them? I tell you that He will avenge them speedily. Nevertheless, when the Son of man comes, will He find faith on the earth?
>
> Luke 18:7-8 (NKJ)

The laying on of hands for healing is essentially a spiritual connection between the person needing God's healing power, the person God is working through, and God. When a believer listens for and follows the Spirit of God, he or she has the potential of being used as a mediator through which God's healing power comes through to a person in need of healing.

> Most assuredly, I say to you, he who believes in Me, the works I do he will do also; and greater works than these he will do, because I go to My Father.
>
> John 14:12 (NKJ)

Healing happens through the will of God. It's done to accomplish His will, and He is still as capable of healing today as He was when Jesus walked this earth.

> Is anyone among you sick? Let him call for the elders of the church, and let them pray over him, anointing him with oil in the name of the Lord. And the prayer of faith will save the sick, and the Lord will raise him up. And if he

has committed sins, he will be forgiven. Confess your trespasses to one another, and pray for one another, that you may be healed. The effective, fervent prayer of a righteous man avails much.

James 5:14-16 (NKJ)

We ask to be prayed over, and the preacher or believers or elders of the church put anointing oil on their hands and touch you while praying over you for Father's will to be done. The key word here is "ask." Many people walk with a "pride" issue and choose not to humble themselves in this way. Anointing oil in, and of itself, does not have supernatural properties. The oil cannot heal or deliver. We experience the power of the use of the oil when we understand in our hearts its message or what it represents in the Bible. It represents different things in different parts of the Bible. In Genesis chapter 28, it says God is with you. In Exodus chapter 40, it says we belong to God and are set apart for His glory. In Isaiah chapter 10, it represents deliverance from bondage. In the New Testament, it represents being anointed with the Holy Spirit working through us to accomplish what Jesus sent Him to accomplish in our lives, healing included, to the praise and glory of God.

> But He was wounded for our transgressions, He was bruised for our iniquities; the chastisement for our peace was upon Him, and by His stripes we are healed.

Isaiah 53:5 (NKJ)

But the act of healing serves more purposes than just the blessing of the person receiving the healing. Healing is a faith builder. It increases the faith of the person being healed. It builds faith in the person the Holy Spirit is working through to bring healing. It builds faith in the people who witness the miracle. And it also builds faith when the testimony of the healing power of God is shared with others.

God's grace empowers the act of healing, and faith is the result. Healing is even one of the gifts of the Spirit that believers receive, as God deems them to, for His purpose. Faith is "believing" in Jesus even though we can't see Him. It takes faith or belief in Jesus just to accept Jesus into our lives as our Savior.

> Now as Jesus passed by, He saw a man who was blind from birth. And His disciples asked Him; saying, "Rabbi, who sinned, this man or his parents, that he was born blind?" Jesus answered, "Neither this man nor his parents sinned, but that the works of God should be revealed in him."
>
> John 9:1-3 (NKJ)

> But what does it say? "The word is near you, in your mouth and in your heart" (that is, the word of faith which we preach), "that if you confess with your mouth the Lord Jesus and believe in your heart that God has raised Him from the dead, you will be saved. For with the heart one believes unto righteousness, and with the mouth confession is made unto salvation."
>
> Romans 10:8-10 (NKJ)

Without faith in things we can't see, how do we believe? How is our name written in the book of life? How would you believe prayers are answered and why would you pray? We build our faith by reading God's word, asking Gods help and direction in prayer, and watching as prayers are answered. Seeing answered prayers in action builds our faith even stronger.

> So then faith comes by hearing and hearing by the word of God.
>
> Romans 10:17 (NKJ)

> Now faith is the substance of things hoped for, the evidence of things not seen. For by it the elders obtained a good testimony. By faith we understand that the worlds

were framed by the word of God, so that the things which are seen were not made of things which are visible.

Hebrews 11:1-3 (NKJ)

But without faith it is impossible to please Him, for he who comes to God must believe that He is, and that He is a rewarder of those who diligently seek Him.

Hebrews 11:6 (NKJ)

Our Father in heaven does things in His time and His way to accomplish His purpose in our lives. And all for the benefit of all His children involved. He does everything for our ultimate good. Building strength and endurance along the way, in order to reach our ultimate goal, which is an eternity in heaven with Him. His grace is enough for all situations.

And we know that all things work together for good to those who love God, to those who are called according to His purpose.

Romans 8:28 (NKJ)

And He said to me, " My grace is sufficient for you, for My strength is made perfect in weakness." Therefore most gladly I will rather boast in my infirmities, that the power of Christ may rest upon me.

2 Corinthians 12:9 (NKJ)

My brethren, count it all joy when you fall into various trials, knowing that the testing of your faith produces patience. But let patience have its perfect work, that you may be perfect and complete, lacking nothing.

James 1:2 (NKJ)

Jesus is the real miracle. He died on the cross for our sins. He accomplished our salvation and victory to overcome this world by His sacrifice on the cross. It is finished! Our part is having faith (belief) in what He has already accomplished for us. When we pray and ask Father for anything we should stand in faith until it manifests in our life or He provides us a different path to serve His divine purpose. Knowing that if it's His will for us to have it, then it will come to pass in His way and His perfect timing for us.

If you would like to look at some biblical testimonies of healing, then check out the book of Matthew to start with: 4:23 and 8:2-3 and 8:5-13 and 8:14-15 and 8:16 and 9:2-7 and 9:20-22 and 9:27-29 and 12:13 and 14:35-36 and 15:28 and 15:30-31 and 17:15-18 and 20:30-34. These are just to start with a few. There are many more as you read the entire Bible.

RESURRECTION OF THE DEAD

The word "faith" is required again in this section. Without faith, how can we even start to believe in resurrection of the dead? We have to first believe that Jesus lived and that He died on the cross while bearing our sins, and He was buried, and that Father raised Him from the tomb on the third day. Resurrection means to bring back to life that which was dead.

> For I delivered to you first of all that which I also received; that Christ died for our sins according to the scriptures, and that He was buried, and that He rose again the third day according to the scriptures, and that He was seen by Cephas then by the twelve. After that He was seen by over five hundred brethren at once, of whom that greater part remain to the present, but some have fallen asleep. After that He was seen by James, then by all the apostles. Then last of all He was seen by me also, as by one born out of due time.
>
> 1 Corinthians 15:3-8 (NKJ)

Now if Christ is preached that He has been raised from the dead, how do some among you say that there is no resurrection of the dead? But if there is no resurrection of the dead, then Christ is not risen. And if Christ is not risen, than our preaching is empty and your faith is also empty.

1 Corinthians 15:12-14 (nkj)

But now Christ is risen from the dead, and has become the first fruits of those who have fallen asleep. For since by man came death, by man also came the resurrection of the dead. For as in Adam all die, even so in Christ all shall be made alive. But each one in his own order: Christ the first fruits, afterward those who are Christ's at His coming.

1 Corinthians 15:20 (nkj)

So also is the resurrection of the dead. The body is sown in corruption, it is raised in incorruption. It is sown in dishonor, it is raised in glory. It is sown in weakness, it is raised in power. It is sown a natural body, it is raised a spiritual body. And so it is written, "The first man Adam became a living being. The last Adam became a life-giving spirit. However, the spiritual is not first, but the natural, and afterward the spiritual. The first man was of the earth, made of dust; the second Man is the Lord from heaven. As was the man of dust, so also are those who are made of dust; and as is the heavenly Man, so also are those who are heavenly. And as we have borne the image of the man of dust, we shall also bear the image of the heavenly Man.

1 Corinthians 15:42 (nkj)

We are not just the fleshly body that you can see. We are made up of body, soul, and spirit. When Adam and Eve sinned against God in the garden and ate of the fruit of knowledge, God separated His spirit from them. God does not dwell in the presence of sin. God sent Jesus to the earth to take our sins from us and reconcile us to Him. Accepting Jesus as our Savior restores our relationship with Him. Our body was created from the earth and He breathed life into us, and through Jesus, His spirit can reside in us again. Our bodies came from the dust of the earth and are sustained by food that comes from the earth. Our spirit came from God and is fed by God's word. When we die, our bodies return to the earth, but our spirit returns to God, then judgment. Prior to death, we will have either accepted Christ Jesus and our names are in the book of life, or we have not accepted Christ Jesus and we are reserved for eternal damnation in hell.

> And as it is appointed for men to die once, but after this the judgment, so Christ was offered once to bear the sins of many. To those who eagerly wait for Him He will appear a second time, apart from sin, for salvation.
>
> Hebrews 9:27-28 (NKJ)

> Therefore by Him let us continually offer the sacrifice of praise to God, that is, the fruit of our lips, giving thanks to His name, but do not forget to do good and to share, for with such sacrifices God is well pleased.
>
> Hebrews 13:15-16 (NKJ)

> Now may the God of peace who brought up our Lord Jesus from the dead, that great Shepherd of the sheep, through the blood of the everlasting covenant, make you complete in every good work to do His will, working in you what is well pleasing in His sight, through Jesus Christ, to whom be glory forever and ever. Amen.
>
> Hebrews 13:20-21 (NKJ)

Other recorded testimonies of resurrection:

> Now it happened; the day after, that He went into a city called Nain; and many of His disciples went with Him, and a large crowd. And when He came near the gate of the city, behold, a dead man was being carried out, the only son of his mother; and she was a widow. And a large crowd from the city was with her. When the Lord saw her, He had compassion on her and said to her, "Do not weep," then He came and touched the open coffin, and those who

carried him stood still. And He said, "Young man, I say to you, arise." So he who was dead sat up and began to speak. And He presented him to his mother. Then fear came upon all, and they glorified God, saying, "A great prophet has risen up among us." And, "God, has visited His people."

Luke 7:11-16 (NKJ)

So it was, when Jesus returned, that the multitude welcomed Him, for they were all waiting for Him. And behold, there came a man named Jairus, and he was a ruler of the synagogue. And he fell down at Jesus' feet and begged Him to come to his house, for he had an only daughter about twelve years of age, and she was dying. But as He went, the multitudes thronged Him.

Luke 8:40-42 (NKJ)

While He was still speaking, someone came from the ruler of the synagogue's house, saying to him, "Your daughter is dead. Do not trouble the Teacher." But when Jesus heard it, He answered him, saying, "Do not be afraid; only believe, and she will be made well." When He came into the house, He permitted no one to go in except Peter, James, and John, and the father and mother of the girl. Now all wept and mourned for her; but He said, "Do not weep; she is not dead, but sleeping." And they ridiculed Him, knowing that she was dead. But He put them all outside, took her by the hand and called, saying, "Little girl, arise." Then her spirit returned, and she arose immediately. And He commanded that she be given something to eat.

Luke 8:49-55 (NKJ)

Then Jesus, again groaning in Himself came to the tomb. It was a cave, and a stone lay against it. Jesus said, "Take away the stone." Martha, the sister of him who was dead, said to Him, "Lord, by this time there is a stench, for he has been dead four days." Jesus said to her, "Did I not say to you that if you would believe you would see the glory of God?" Then they took away the stone from the place where the dead man was lying. And Jesus lifted up His eyes and said, "Father, I thank You that You have heard Me. And I know that You always hear Me, but because of the people who are standing by I said this, that they may believe that You sent Me." Now when He had said these things, He cried with a loud voice, "Lazarus, come forth!" And he who had died came out bound hand and foot with grave clothes, and his face was wrapped with a cloth. Jesus said to them, "Loose him, and let him go." Then many of the Jews who had come to Mary and had seen the things Jesus did, believed in Him.

John 11:38-45 (NKJ)

LIFE OR DEATH CHOICES

LIFE VS DEATH

SOME CHURCHES TODAY will not include these topics in their teachings. The truth of God's word is being cast down by many, revised or changed so as not to scare people away. The truth is scary if you're not in line with God's word. Church groups are actually replacing God's word with a watered down gospel that lacks power to work a spiritual transformation in their congregation. Lack of the true word is causing us to be led astray by fables. Many churches don't want to talk about hell because their congregation may become upset with the reality of it. Some won't talk about the Holy Spirit or even Jesus. When Jesus walked the earth and taught the gospel, He mentioned hell, hades, sheol, the bottomless pit, etc. He loved us so much that He wanted us to know the truth and to choose life instead of death, an eternity in heaven with Him instead of an eternity of fire and total separation from everyone. God created us with a free will to choose. He wanted a people that choose to love Him as He loves us.

> I call heaven and earth as witnesses today against you, that I have set before you life and death, blessing and cursing; therefore choose life that both you and your descendants may live; that you may love the Lord your God, that

you may obey His voice, and that you may cling to Him, for He is your life and the length of your days; and that you may dwell in the land which the Lord swore to your fathers, to Abraham, Isaac, and Jacob to give them.

Deuteronomy 30:19-20 (NKJ)

For God so loved the world that He gave His only begotten Son, that whoever believes in Him should not perish but have everlasting life. For God did not send His Son into the world to condemn the world, but that the world through Him might be saved. He who believes in Him is not condemned; but he who does not believe is condemned already, because he has not believed in the name of the only begotten Son of God.

John 3:16 (NKJ)

God is a just God. He puts a hunger in our hearts for Him, at some point in each person's life, and every person that seeks for Him will find Him.

For the wrath of God is revealed from heaven against all ungodliness and unrighteousness of men, who suppress the truth in unrighteousness, because what may be known of God is manifest in them, for God has shown it to them. For since the creation of the world His invisible attributes are clearly seen, being understood by the things that are made, even His eternal power and Godhead, so that they are without excuse.

Romans 1:18-20 (NKJ)

I love those who love Me, and those who seek Me diligently will find Me.

Proverbs 8:17 (NKJ)

And you will seek Me and find Me, when you search for Me with all your heart.

Jeremiah 29:13 (NKJ)

Ask me and it will be given to you, seek, and you will find; knock, and it will be opened to you. For everyone who asks receives, and he who seeks finds, and to him who knocks it will be opened. Or what man is there among you who if his son asks for bread, will give him a stone? Or if he asks for a fish, will he give him a serpent? If you then, being evil, know how to give good gifts to your children, how much more will your Father who is in heaven give good things to those who ask Him!

Matthew 7:7-11 (NKJ)

And He has made from one blood every nation of men to dwell on all the face of the earth, and has determined their appointed times and the boundaries of their dwellings, so that they should seek the Lord, in the hope that they might grope for Him and find Him, though He is not far from each one of us; for in Him we live and move and have our being, as also some of your own poets have said, "For we are also His offspring."

Acts 17:26-28 (NKJ)

God is a loving God. He provides a way for us to be reconciled to Him and reestablish the personal relationship that He designed from the beginning of mankind. He does not send people to hell, but because of our free will to choose, people are sending themselves to hell. Hell was not originally created for people. It was created for Satan and the fallen angels and then had to be enlarged. God's Son was not sent so people would be sent to hell. He was sent to bring us back to our Father who loves us.

The Lord is not slack concerning His promise, as some count slackness, but is longsuffering toward us, not willing that any should perish but that all should come to repentance.

2 Peter 3:9 (NKJ)

That is, that God was in Christ reconciling the world to Himself, not imputing their trespasses to them, and has committed to us the word of reconciliation.

2 Corinthians 5:19 (NKJ)

Then He will also say to those on the left hand, "Depart from Me, you cursed, into the everlasting fire prepared for the devil and his angels."

Matthew 25:41 (NKJ)

Therefore My people have gone into captivity, because they have no knowledge; their honorable men are famished, and their multitude dried up with thirst therefore sheol has enlarged itself and opened its mouth beyond measure; their glory and their multitude and their pomp, and he who is jubilant shall descend into it.

Isaiah 5:13-14 (NKJ)

It's not about Him rejecting us. The real question here is, "How can anyone reject a loving God?" The devil is the father of lies and loves to destroy people's lives and blame God. The truth is that God loved us so much that He made the ultimate sacrifice to bring us back to Himself through His Son Jesus Christ our Savior.

"Come now, and let us reason together," says the Lord, "though your sins are like scarlet, they shall be as white as snow; though they are red like crimson, they shall be as wool." "If you are willing and obedient, you shall eat the good of the land; but if you refuse and rebel, you shall be devoured by the sword," for the mouth of the Lord has spoken.

Isaiah 1:18-20 (NKJ)

They profess to know God, but in works they deny Him, being abominable, disobedient, and disqualified for every good work.

Titus 1:16 (NKJ)

For the wages of sin is death, but the gift of God is eternal life in Christ Jesus our Lord.

Romans 6:23 (NKJ)

If we say that we have fellowship with Him, and walk in darkness, we lie and do not practice the truth. But if we walk in the light as He is in the light we have fellowship with one another, and the blood of Jesus Christ His Son cleanses us from all sin. If we say that we have no sin, we deceive ourselves, and the truth is not in us. If we confess our sins, He is faithful and just to forgive us our sins and to cleanse us from all unrighteousness.

1 John 1:6-9 (NKJ)

When we share information about eternal choices, it is literally a life or death matter. If you truly care about the family and friends around you, why would you not share Jesus with them? One of the sermons I listened to likened sharing information about "Jesus and salvation" to the act of "pulling people out of a burning building or house fire." Just because you do not see them literally walking on the edge of a lake of fire doesn't mean the situation isn't that serious. None of us know the day or time we will be called home, and when I am called home, I want to know I did all I could to make sure I would see my friends and family again. People usually don't realize how easy it is to receive salvation. So make sure when you talk to them that they know:

- It's not based on works (nothing they can do to earn it)

- It's a free gift (Jesus already paid it all on the cross)

- It's easy to receive—believe that Jesus lived and died and was raised back up "resurrected" by God. Confess that you're a sinner and receive Jesus as your savior.

For by grace you have been saved through faith, and that not of yourself, it is the gift of God.

Ephesians 2:8 (NKJ)

For the wages of sin is death, but the gift of God is eternal life in Christ Jesus our Lord.

Romans 6:23 (NKJ)

That if you confess with your mouth the Lord Jesus and believe in your heart that God has raised Him from the dead, you will be saved. For with the heart one believes unto righteousness and with the mouth confession is made unto salvation.

Romans 10:9 (NKJ)

HEAVEN VS HELL

It's also important to know what the Bible says about heaven and hell so you can set the record straight when people start asking you questions based on some movie they may have seen or false statements they may have heard. The devil would want you to think that hell is one big fun and never-ending party where the sky's the limit and anything goes. The devil would also have you think that heaven is one of the most boring places you could ever imagine where everyone has to be serious and no one has any fun. So let's look at scripture and find out what the truth of the matter is.

FACTS ABOUT HEAVEN

When we die, our fleshly bodies return to the dust of the earth, but our spirit and soul go either to heaven or hell until the return of Jesus, when our bodies will be resurrected from the grave. Traditionally, we bury people based on the scriptures with their heads to the west and their feet to the east so they will be facing Jesus when they are raised from the grave.

For as the lightning comes from the east and flashes to the west, so also will the coming of the Son of Man be.

Matthew 24:27 (NKJ)

These are the facts:

1. We will have resurrected bodies, and we can eat food.

The first man was of the earth, made of dust; the second Man is the Lord from heaven. As was the man of dust, so also are those who are made of dust; and as is the heavenly Man, so also are those who are heavenly, and as we have borne the image of the man of dust, we shall also bear the image of the heavenly Man.

1 Corinthians 15:47-49 (NKJ)

In the middle of its street, and on either side of the river, was the tree of life, which bore twelve fruits, each tree yielding its fruit every month. The leaves of the tree were for the healing of the nations.

Revelation 22:2 (NKJ)

2. Believers will go immediately to heaven when they die.

We are confident, yes, well pleased rather to be absent from the body and to be present with the Lord.

2 Corinthians 5:8 (NKJ)

Then he said to Jesus, "Lord, remember me when You come into Your kingdom." And Jesus said to him, "Assuredly, I say to you, today you will be with Me in Paradise."

Luke 23:42-43 (NKJ)

3. We will be able to talk to one another, and we will remember things that happened to us on earth.

When He opened the fifth seal, I saw under the altar the souls of those who had been slain for the Word of God and for the testimony which they held. And they cried with a loud voice, saying, "How long, O Lord, holy and true, until You judge and avenge our blood on those who dwell on the earth?"

Revelation 6:9-11 (NKJ)

4. We do have emotions in heaven.

I say to you that likewise there will be more joy in heaven over one sinner who repents than over ninety-nine just persons who need no repentance.

Luke 15:7 (NKJ)

5. We will know what's happening on earth.

Therefore we also, since we are surrounded by so great a cloud of witnesses, let us lay aside every weight, and the sin which so easily ensnares us, and let us run with endurance the race that is set before us.

Hebrews 12:1 (NKJ)

6. It will not be boring. There will be lots of new things to explore and learn about. Plus, no more tears, death, sorrow, crying, or pain.

Now I saw a new heaven and a new earth for the first heaven and the first earth had passed away. Also there was no more sea. Then I, John, saw the holy city, New Jerusalem, coming down out of heaven from God, prepared as a bride adorned for her husband. And I heard a loud voice from heaven saying, "Behold, the tabernacle of God is with men, and He will dwell with them, and they shall be His people. God Himself will be with them and be their God. And God will wipe away every tear from their eyes; there shall be no more pain, for the former things have passed away." Then He who sat on the throne said, "Behold, I make all things new." And He said to me, "Write, for these words are true and faithful."

Revelation 21:1-5 (NKJ)

And He said to me, "It is done! I Am the Alpha and the Omega, the Beginning and the End. I will give of the fountain of the water of life freely to him who thirsts."

Revelation 21:6 (NKJ)

And the Spirit and the bride say, "Come!" And let him who hears say, "Come!" And let him who thirsts come. Whoever desires, let him take the water of life freely!

Revelation 22:17 (NKJ)

That if you confess with your mouth the Lord Jesus and believe in your heart that God raised Him from the dead, you will be saved.

Romans 10:9 (NKJ)

For "whoever calls on the name of the Lord shall be saved."

Romans 10:13 (NKJ)

7. All those who believe and receive Jesus will be there, and we will have animals for our enjoyment. Not the same ones we had on earth but newly created ones for us to enjoy.

The wolf also shall dwell with the lamb, the leopard shall lie down with the young goat, the calf and the young lion and the fatling together; and a little child shall lead them. The cow and the bear shall graze; their young ones shall lie down together; and the lion shall eat straw like the ox. The nursing child shall play by the cobra's hole, and the weaned child shall put his hand in the viper's den. They shall not hurt nor destroy in all My holy mountain, for the earth shall be full of the knowledge of the Lord as the waters cover the sea.

Isaiah 11:6-9 (NKJ)

FACTS ABOUT HELL

Jesus gives a description of what hell is like when he tells the story about Lazarus. Jesus talked about hell a lot so people would get an understanding of what it is like and choose not to go there. Many people believe this story to be a parable, but Jesus did not say it was a parable. He did not say "it is like this or that," but He stated the facts of the story very plainly.

> There was a certain rich man clothed in purple and fine linen and fared sumptuously every day. But there was a certain beggar named Lazarus, full of sores, who laid at his gate; desiring to be fed with the crumbs which fell from the rich mans table. More over the dogs came and licked his sores. So it was that the beggar died, and was carried by the angels to Abraham's bosom. The rich man also died and was buried. And being *in torments in Hades,* he lifted up his eyes and saw Abraham afar off, and Lazarus in his bosom. Then he cried and said, "Father Abraham, have mercy on me, and send Lazarus that he may dip the tip of his finger in water and cool my tongue; for *I am tormented in this flame.*" But Abraham said, "Son, remember that in your life time you received your good things, and like wise Lazarus evil things; but now he is comforted and you are tormented. And besides all this, between us and you there is *a great gulf fixed,* so that those who want to pass from here to you cannot, nor can those from there pass to us." Then he said, "I beg you therefore, father, that you would send him to my fathers house, for I have five brothers, that he may testify to them, lest they also come to *this place of torment.*" Abraham said to him, "They have Moses and the prophets; let them hear them." And he said, "No, father Abraham; but if one goes to them from the dead, they will repent." But he said to him, "If they do not hear Moses and the prophets, neither will they be persuaded though one rise from the dead."

> Luke 16:19-31 (NKJ)

Then He will also say to those on the left hand, "Depart from Me you cursed into the *everlasting fire* prepared for the devil and his angels."

Matthew 25:41 (NKJ)

These are the facts:

- Hell is full of torments and torture (pain).

- Hell has a great fixed gulf from heaven that people can't cross back or forth from.

- Hell is everlasting fire prepared for the devil and his angels.

- Hell was enlarged to accommodate the number of unbelievers.

Therefore my people have gone into captivity, because they have no knowledge, their honorable men are famished, and their multitude dried up with thirst. Therefore sheol (hell) has enlarged itself and opened its mouth beyond measure; their glory and their multitude and their pomp, and he who is jubilant, shall descend into it.

Isaiah 5:13-14 (NKJ)

Hell is called outer darkness (no light there). Being able to see and feel things keeps our minds sane. There will be no light in the utter darkness.

But the sons of the kingdom will be cast out into outer darkness. There will be weeping and gnashing of teeth.

Matthew 8:12 (NKJ)

Hell is a lake of fire and brimstone (after judgment/second death).

He who overcomes shall inherit all things, and I will be his God and he shall be My son. But the cowardly, unbelieving, abominable, murderers, sexually immoral, sorcerers, idolators and all liars shall have their part in the lake which burns with fire and brimstone, which is the second death.

Revelation 21:7-8 (NKJ)

Hell is a bottomless pit—not able to touch solid things. Again, being able to feel solid things helps keep us sane.

And he opened the bottomless pit, and smoke arose out of the pit like the smoke of a great furnace. So the sun and the air were darkened because of the smoke of the pit.

Revelation 9:2 (NKJ)

When they finished their testimony, the beast that ascends out of the bottomless pit will make war against them, overcome them, and kill them.

Revelation 11:7 (NKJ)

The beast that you saw was, and is not, and will ascend out of the bottomless pit and go to perdition. And those who dwell on the earth will marvel, whose names are not written in the Book of Life from the foundation of the world, when they see the beast that was, and is not, and yet is.

Revelation 17:8 (NKJ)

And He cast him into the bottomless pit, and shut him up, and set a seal on him, so that he should deceive the nations no more till the thousand years were finished. But after these things he must be released for a little while.

Revelation 20:3 (NKJ)

In hell, there is no rest day or night (no peace). Rest and hope are two emotions that also keep us sane. Hopelessness is one of the tactics Satan uses to convince people to commit suicide.

"And the smoke of their torment ascends forever and ever; and they have no rest day or night, who worship the beast and his image, and whoever receives the mark of his name."

Revelation 14:11 (NKJ)

ETERNAL JUDGMENT AND REWARDS

It matters how we live and behave while we are on earth. Your belief will determine where you spend eternity and your behavior will determine how you spend eternity. We actually get to pick which judgment we attend. If you accept Jesus and become a believer, then you are "judged by your works." If you do not accept Jesus as your Savior, "you are judged by your sins." God is a just God so there will be degrees of rewards and degrees of punishment.

> Then the Lord knows how to deliver the godly out of temptations and to reserve the unjust under punishment for the day of judgment.
>
> 2 Peter 2:9 (NKJ)

> But the heavens and the earth which are now preserved by the same word, are reserved for fire until the day of judgment and perdition of ungodly men.
>
> 2 Peter 3:7 (NKJ)

Perdition is a state of eternal punishment and damnation into which a sinful and unrepentant person passes after death.

> But I say to you that for every idle word men may speak, they will give account of it in the day of judgment.
>
> Matthew 12:36 (NKJ)

> And as it is appointed for men to die once, but after this the judgment.
>
> Hebrews 9:27 (NKJ)

For God will bring every work into judgment, including every secret thing, whether good or evil.

Ecclesiastes 12:14 (NKJ)

JUDGMENT SEAT OF CHRIST

The judgment seat of Christ is when all believers give account of the works they accomplished for the kingdom. There are rewards.

Therefore we make it our aim, whether present or absent, to be well pleasing to Him. For we must all appear before the judgment seat of Christ, that each one may receive the things done in the body, according to what he has done, whether good or bad.

2 Corinthians 5:9-10 (NKJ)

For the Son of Man will come in the glory of His Father with His angels, and then He will reward each according to his works.

Matthew 16:27 (NKJ)

And behold, I am coming quickly, and My reward is with Me, to give everyone according to his work.

Revelation 22:12 (NKJ)

And if you call on the Father, who without partiality judges *according to each ones works*, conduct yourselves throughout the time of your stay here in fear.

1 Peter 1:17 (NKJ)

For by grace you have been saved through faith, and that not of ourselves; it is the gift of God, not of works, lest anyone should boast. For we are His workmanship, *created in Christ Jesus for good works,* which God prepared before hand that we should walk in them.

Ephesians 2:8-10 (NKJ)

But why do you judge your brother? Or why do you show contempt for your brother? For we shall all stand before the judgment seat of Christ.

Romans 14:10 (NKJ)

Take heed that you do not do your charitable deeds before men, to be seen by them. Otherwise, you have no reward from your Father in heaven.

Matthew 6:1 (NKJ)

And now, little children, abide in Him, that when He appears, we may have confidence and not be ashamed before Him at His coming.

1 John 2:28 (NKJ)

Do not lay up for yourselves treasures on earth, where moth and rust destroy and where thieves break in and steal; but lay up for yourselves treasures in heaven where neither moth nor rust destroys and where thieves do not break in and steal. For where your treasure is, there your heart will be also.

Matthew 6:19-21 (NKJ)

I pause to ask you this:

- What is important to you? Things or People?
- So what are we doing for the kingdom?
- Are we wasting our lives or following and serving Jesus?
- Will we be ashamed before Jesus when we see Him?
- The good works we do accomplish for the kingdom, are we humbly helping others and sharing the gospel of Jesus or do we boast and brag about being a good Christian and the mighty works we do to receive praise and higher status from those around us?

- God sees all. He is a just God. He searches the hearts of men and is a rewarder of the humble and faithful. How is your heart?

When Jesus returns, all the dead in Christ will be resurrected from the grave, and the rest of the believers, still alive on earth at that time, will be caught up with them to heaven. This is the first resurrection. We will be with Jesus!

> For the Lord Himself will descend from heaven with a shout, with the voice of an archangel, and with the trumpet of God. And the dead in Christ will rise first. Then we who are alive and remain shall be caught up together with them in the clouds to meet the Lord in the air. And thus we shall always be with the Lord.
>
> 1 Thessalonians 4:16-17 (NKJ)

GREAT WHITE THRONE JUDGMENT

The Great White Throne judgment is talked about in Revelation. It's where the non-believers are called forth, their bodies being resurrected from the grave (which is the second resurrection) to meet at the Great White Throne. I plead with you to stay in good standing with God, and if you're not sure if you're saved or not, surrender everything to the King Jesus right now! You do not want to take part in the wrath of God or eternal damnation. Once you die on this earth, it's too late to change your mind. Your eternal destination at death is set (we are not promised tomorrow!). How you live and behave on earth matters!

> Then I saw a great white throne and Him who sat on it, from whose face the earth and the heavens fled away. And there was found no place for them. And I saw the dead, small and great, standing before God, and books were opened (works / deeds). And another book was opened, which is the Book of Life. And the dead were judged according to their works, by the things which were written

in the books. The sea gave up the dead who were in it, and death and hades delivered up the dead who were in them. And they were judged, each one according to his works. Then death and hades were cast into the lake of fire. This is the second death. And anyone not found written in the Book of Life was cast into the lake of fire.

Revelation 20:11-15 (NKJ)

Woe to you Chorazin! Woe to you, Bethsaida! For if the mighty works which were done in you had been done in Tyre and Sidon, they would have repented long ago in sack cloth and ashes. But I say to you, it will be more tolerable for Tyre and Sidon in the day of judgment than for you.

Matthew 11:21-22 (NKJ)

But in accordance with your hardness and your impenitent heart you are treasuring up for yourself wrath in the day of wrath and revelation of the righteous judgment of God.

Romans 2:5 (NKJ)

As scripture indicates above, there are degrees of wrath or punishment. When Jesus was teaching the gospel in Capernaum, He said,

"And you, Capernaum, who are exalted to heaven, will be brought down to hades; for if the mighty works which were done in you had been done in Sodom, it would have remained until this day. But I say to you that it shall be more tolerable for the land of Sodom in the day of judgment than for you."

Matthew 11:23-24 (NKJ)

The days of Sodom happened during the Old Testament times, and they did not experience the miracles that Jesus worked. But Capernaum did see Jesus work miracles, and they still rejected Him. Jesus is a permanent cure for suffering and death, but He is still rejected by people in today's times.

Salvation is a free gift from God. Jesus died to pay the price for all of our sins once and for all. All we have to do is believe this in our hearts, speak the words of accepting Jesus into our hearts, admit we are sinners, and repent of our sins and He washes us clean! God's grace empowers us to live for Him. We can't do it on our own, we surrender to Him, and He empowers us to change. He transforms us!

WHAT ABOUT THE RETURN OF JESUS?

There are so many different doctrines/beliefs on this topic and the discussion of the rapture and "when" it will all take place. There are all kinds of fancy theology words like pre-trib rapture, mid-trib rapture, and post-trib rapture. But does the time of occurrence really matter? Or is it more important how we spend our time on earth before His return? No one knows the day or time. Not even the angels in heaven! The main thing is to not get side tracked by things happening in the world. Stay focused on the mission at hand which is sharing the gospel of Christ and steps of salvation, which are literally life and death matters!

> But of that day and hour no one knows, not even the angels of heaven, but My Father only.
>
> Matthew 24:36 (NKJ)

> Therefore you also be ready, for the Son of Man is coming at an hour you do not expect.
>
> Matthew 24:44 (NKJ)

> And Jesus answered and said to them, "Take heed that no one deceives you. For many will come in My name, saying "I am the Christ," and will deceive many.
>
> Matthew 24:4-5 (NKJ)

****Do Business Till I Come!**** Stay on track. Follow the will of God for your life!

Lets look at the parable of the minas to examine what we should be doing.

> A certain nobleman went into a far country to receive for himself a kingdom and to return. So he called ten of his servants, delivered to them ten minas and said to them, "Do business till I come" But his citizens hated him, and sent a delegation after him saying, "We will not have this man to reign over us." And so it was that when he returned, having received the kingdom, he then commanded these servants, to whom he had given the money, to be called to him, that he might know how much every man had gained by trading. Then came the first, saying, "Master, your mina has earned ten minas." And he said to him, "Well done, good servant; because you were faithful in a very little, have authority over ten cities. And the second came, saying, "Master, your mina has earned five minas;" likewise he said to him, "You also be over five cities." Then another came, saying, "Master, here is your mina, which I have kept put away in a handkerchief. For I feared you, because you are an austere man. You collect what you did not deposit, and reap what you did not sow." And he said to him, "Out of your own mouth I will judge you, you wicked servant. You knew that I was an austere man, collecting what I did not deposit and reaping what I did not sow. Why then did you not put my money in the bank, that at my coming I might have collected it with interest?" And he said to those who stood by, "Take the mina from him and give it to him who has ten minas! (But they said to him "Master, he has ten minas.") "For I say to you, that to every one who has will be given; and from him who does not have, even what he has will be taken away from him. But bring here those enemies of mine, who did not want me to reign over them, and slay them before me."

> Luke 19:12-27 (NKJ)

If you look at this parable from a kingdom perspective, you'll see that the nobleman or master represents Jesus. He ascended into heaven to receive His kingdom and is returning again. The servants are the believers, and He entrusts us with the stewardship of His people who are the real treasure on this earth. "Do business till I come" should be about taking care of each other: witnessing to bring about salvation, giving to the church to help support bringing the word of God to the people, serving to help each other both directly, and indirectly volunteering in church events and the community, fund raising to feed and clothe those in need, and just loving people in general. The list of opportunities is so much bigger than this.

The citizens in the parable are the non-believers who reject Christ and as He says in verse 27, they will face eternal judgment. Sure wouldn't want to be in that category. When Jesus returns, all believers will be caught up to meet Him in the clouds, and we will face the judgment seat of Christ. Every work will be brought into judgment both good and bad, and He will reward according to each one's works.

Remember, your behavior determines how you spend eternity, and Jesus is returning with His rewards. Everyday is one day closer to His return, and there is still so much work to be done. Time is of the essence.

> Then He said to His disciples, "The harvest truly is plentiful, but the labors are few. Therefore pray the Lord of the harvest to send out laborers into His harvest."
>
> Matthew 9:37 (NKJ)

It's life or death decision time. There are so many that will perish if they don't hear and accept the truth about salvation. Faith (belief) is the key that changes things, and the Bible is the direction book. People are the real treasure we are talking about. Everything else on this earth will pass away at the designated time. We should stay focused on the task at hand "salvation" and "Do business till I come."

News Flash: The enemy wants you to get sidetracked!

> And they overcame him by the blood of the Lamb and by the word of their testimony, and they did not love their lives to the death.
>
> Revelation 12:11 (NKJ)

> For you yourselves, know perfectly that the day of the Lord so comes as a thief in the night. For when they say, "Peace and Safety!" then sudden destruction comes upon them, as labor pains upon a pregnant woman. And they shall not escape. But you, brethren, are not in darkness, so that this day should overtake you as a thief.
>
> 1 Thessalonians 5:2-4 (NKJ)

> And if I go and prepare a place for you, I will come again and receive you to Myself; that where I am, there you may be also.
>
> John 14:3 (NKJ)

> Blessed are those servants whom the Master, when He comes, will find watching. Assuredly, I say to you that He will gird Himself and have them sit down to eat, and will come and serve them.
>
> Luke 12:37 (NKJ)

> Who also said, " Men of Galilee, why do you stand gazing up into heaven? This same Jesus, who was taken up from you into heaven, will so come in like manner as you saw Him go into heaven."
>
> Acts 1:11 (NKJ)

> And in that day His feet will stand on the Mount of Olives. Which faces Jerusalem on the east. And the Mount of Olives shall be split in two, from east to west, making a very large valley; half of the mountain shall move toward the north and half of it toward the south.
>
> Zachariah 14:4 (NKJ)

And to give you who are troubled rest with us when the Lord Jesus is revealed from heaven with His mighty angels, in flaming fire taking vengeance on those who do not know God, and on those who do not obey the gospel of our Lord Jesus Christ.

Matthew 24:31

Then the sign of the Son of Man will appear in heaven, and then all the tribes of the earth will mourn, and they will see the Son of Man coming on the clouds of heaven with power and great glory. And He will send His angels with a great sound of a trumpet, and they will gather together His elect from the four winds, from one end of heaven to the other.

2 Thessalonians 1:7-8 (NKJ)

And then the lawless one will be revealed, who the Lord will consume with the breath of His mouth and destroy with the brightness of His coming.

2 Thessalonians 2:8 (NKJ)

He will be great, and will be called the Son of the Highest; and the Lord God will give Him the throne of His father David.

Luke 1:32 (NKJ)

All nations will be gathered before Him, and He will separate them one from another, as a shepherd divides his sheep from the goats.

Matthew 25:32 (NKJ)

"Behold the days are coming" says the Lord, "That I will raise to David a Branch of Righteousness; a King shall reign and prosper, and execute judgment and righteousness in the earth."

Jeremiah 23:5 (NKJ)

Then the seventh angel sounded: And there were loud voices in heaven, saying "The kingdoms of this world have become the kingdoms of our Lord and of His Christ, and He shall reign forever and ever!"

Revelation 11:15 (NKJ)

Then to Him was given dominion and glory and a kingdom, that all peoples, nations, and languages should serve Him. His dominion is an everlasting dominion, which shall not pass away, and His kingdom the one which shall not be destroyed.

Daniel 7:14 (NKJ)

Do not marvel at this; for the hour is coming in which all who are in the graves will hear His voice and come forth – those who have done good, to the resurrection of life, and those who have done evil, to the resurrection of condemnation.

John 5:28-29 (NKJ)

Behold, He is coming with clouds, and every eye will see Him, even they who pierced Him. And all the tribes of the earth will mourn because of Him. Even so, Amen.

Revelation 1:7 (NKJ)

Therefore God also has highly exalted Him and given Him the name which is above every name, that at the name of Jesus every knee should bow, of those in heaven, and of those on earth, and of those under the earth, and that every tongue should confess that Jesus Christ is Lord, to the glory of God the Father.

Philippians 2:9-11 (NKJ)

Look to Me, and be saved, all you ends of the earth! For I Am God, and there is no other. I have sworn by Myself; the word has gone out of My mouth in righteousness, and shall not return, that to Me every knee shall bow, every tongue shall take an oath.

Isaiah 45:22-23 (NKJ)

We can even hasten His return!!!!

Looking for and hastening the coming of the day of God, because of which the heavens will be dissolved, being on fire, and the elements will melt with fervent heat?

2 Peter 3:12 (NKJ)

And this gospel of the kingdom will be preached in all the world as a witness to all the nations, and then the end will come.

Matthew 24:14 (NKJ)

THE POWER OF WORDS

WORDS BUILD AND words tear down. It's important to realize how powerful the words you speak are and the far-reaching effects your spoken words have on the lives of the people around you. God's word says, "Out of the abundance of your heart, your mouth speaks." We can only hide behind a false facade for so long before the light shines in the dark places and exposes all truth. We should ask God to search our hearts and ask Him to set things right. He already knows what's in our hearts, and He waits for us to ask, so He can lovingly and patiently bring our deepest hurts and secrets to light. As we surrender them to Him, He heals us and sets us free as only He can. It's a process of surrender and transformation. As we are transformed, our hearts change, and as we feed on His word, our way of seeing or understanding changes. His truth is revealed by the Holy Spirit, and the Holy Spirit working through us positively affects the lives of other people around us by what we speak from our hearts.

> Therefore I say to you, every sin and blasphemy will be forgiven men, but the blasphemy against the Spirit will not be forgiven men. Anyone who speaks a word against the Son of Man, it will be forgiven him, but whoever speaks against the Holy Spirit, it will not be forgiven him, either in this age or in the age to come. Either make the tree

good and its fruit good, or else make the tree bad and its fruit bad, for a tree is known by its fruit. "Brood of vipers! How can you, being evil speak good things? For out of the abundance of the heart the mouth speaks. A good man out of the good treasure of his heart brings forth good things. But I say to you that for every idle word men may speak, they will give account of it in the day of judgment. For by your words you will be justified, and by your words you will be condemned.

Matthew 12:31-37 (NKJ)

I had an eye-opening experience when I was learning about the power of spoken words and the condition of my heart. I actually had a dream one morning that changed my perspective on things I was doing. The dream went like this: *I was in a gathering place with food and music and people I knew ran up to me and started talking about another person we were acquainted with. They went on and on about the dirty details of what had just happened to her with all the "can you believe that's" and "if I was her's" and "what was she thinking's," and I just stood and listened and nodded my head every now and then without being directly involved in the conversation and not even saying a word in response. After a minute or two, they all left the area, and that's when I heard a crying coming from behind me in the dark back corner. The person they had been talking about had heard everything and was totally embarrassed and heartbroken and alone. And that's when a veil dropped between the visible and spiritual world and Father and Jesus and Holy Spirit and the angels of heaven were watching.* At this point, I woke up and was crying really hard and repenting. I had been just standing there listening to them and being proud of myself for not getting involved in their gossip and backbiting and didn't even try to defend the person they were talking about or establish Jesus's view of what they were doing as being wrong. That's when Father spoke to my heart and said that, sometimes, doing nothing at all is actually condoning or agreeing with what they are doing. We have to take a stand for what's right, and we certainly aren't safe riding the fence or remaining silent. God is love! We are to love God and love others. It's that simple.

It's time to search your heart. Ask God to search you and show you anything that displeases Him. Even just kidding or joking can still hurt people.

> A man's stomach shall be satisfied from the fruit of his mouth, from the produce of his lips he shall be filled. Death and life are in the power of the tongue, and those who love it will eat its fruit.
>
> Proverbs 18:20-21 (NKJ)

Words can bring life or death to any relationship. We are citizens of God's Kingdom living by His standards not by the world's standards of what is acceptable. Our words should be encouraging to each other to build each other up, not discouraging or condemning.

> Set a guard, O Lord, over my mouth, keep watch over the door of my lips.
>
> Psalm 141:3 (NKJ)

> I said, "I will guard my ways lest I sin with my tongue, I will restrain my mouth with a muzzle, while the wicked are before me."
>
> Psalm 39:1 (NKJ)

> These six things the Lord hates, yes, seven are an abomination to Him, a proud look, a lying tongue, hands that shed innocent blood, a heart that devises wicked plans, feet that are swift in running to evil, a false witness who speaks lies, and one who sows discord among brethren.
>
> Proverbs 6:16-19 (NKJ)

What does God's word say about slanderers and gossipers and trouble-makers?

But avoid foolish disputes, genealogies, contentions, and strivings about the law, for they are unprofitable and useless. Reject a devise man after the first and second admonition, knowing that such a person is warped and sinning being self-condemned.

Titus 3:9-11 (NKJ)

He also says to not be a talebearer, breaking someone's trust when they told you something in confidence. Keep their secrets so they can trust you when they need help. By all means, don't use the "I'm telling you so you can pray for them" line as an excuse to spread hurtful information. Check your heart and share with people that will pray with you for the person and not just gossip about the person. The exception would be if someone were planning to intentionally and physically hurt themselves or others, then you would seek appropriate help.

He who goes about as talebearer reveals secrets, therefore do not associate with one who flatters with his lips.

Proverbs 20:19 (NKJ)

But now I have written to you not to keep company with anyone named a brother, who is sexually immoral, or covetous, or an idolater, or a reviler, or a drunkard, or an extortioner, not even to eat with such a person.

1 Corinthians 5:11 (NKJ)

But now you yourselves are to put off all these: anger, wrath, malice, blasphemy, filthy language out of your mouth.

Colossians 3:8 (NKJ)

If Christ is all and in all, then what we are saying and doing to each other, are we not also saying and doing to Christ?

For you are all sons of God through faith in Christ Jesus. For as many of you as were baptized into Christ have put on Christ. There is neither Jew nor Greek, there is neither slave nor free, there is neither male nor female; for you are all one in Christ Jesus.

Galatians 3:26-28 (NKJ)

Let no corrupt word proceed out of your mouth, but what is good for necessary edification, that it may impart grace to the hearers. And do not grieve the Holy Spirit of God by whom you were sealed for the day of redemption. Let all bitterness, wrath, anger, clamor, and evil speaking be put away from you, with all malice. And be kind to one another, tenderhearted, forgiving one another, even as God in Christ forgave you.

Ephesians 4:29-31 (NKJ)

Therefore be imitators of God as dear children. And walk in love, as Christ also has loved us and given Himself for us, an offering and a sacrifice to God for a sweet smelling aroma.

Ephesians 5:1-2 (NKJ)

It is literally a daily task to consciously yield your tongue to the Holy Spirit each day!

Indeed we put bits in horses mouths that they may obey us, and we turn their whole body. Look also at ships. Although they are so large and driven by fierce winds, they are turned by a very small rudder wherever the pilot desires. Even so the tongue is a little member and boasts great things. See how great a forest a little fire kindles? And the tongue is a fire, a world of iniquity. The tongue is so set among our members that it defiles the whole body, and sets on fire the course of nature; and it is set on fire by hell.

James 3:3-6 (NKJ)

But no man can tame the tongue. It is an unruly evil, full of deadly poison. With it we bless our God and Father, and

with it we curse men, who have been made in the simili-
tude of God. Out of the same mouth proceed blessings and
cursing. My brethren, these things ought not be so.

James 3:8-10 (NKJ)

In the book of Acts chapter 2, when the Day of Pentecost had
come and the Holy Spirit fell on them and filled them, the first
thing He took control of was the tongue.

And they were all filled with the Holy Spirit and began
to speak with other tongues, as the Spirit gave them
utterance.

Acts 2:4 (NKJ)

The tongue produces life or death. Satan also tries to get control of your thoughts and your tongue so he can use it to speak
destruction to yourselves and others. That is why it's so important to yield our tongue to the Holy Spirit and keep our minds
focused on God and His word. As we stay surrendered to God
and meditate on His word, we learn how to use our words to
bless others and in turn produce good fruit by speaking the truth
of His word.

God created with His word, and we have the ability to come
into agreement with the Creator. We should make our spoken
words line up with God. Speak the truth, and don't exaggerate
or make it bigger than it is. What comes out of our mouth, the
words we speak, directly affect the quality of our life.

But what does it say? "The word is near you, in your
mouth and in your heart (that is, the word of faith which
we preach), that if you confess with your mouth the Lord
Jesus and believe in your heart that God raised Him from
the dead, you will be saved."

Romans 10:8-9 (NKJ)

> A good man out of the good treasure of his heart brings
> forth good things, and an evil man out of the evil treasure
> brings forth evil things.
>
> Matthew 12:35 (NKJ)

Concentrate on speaking life into the kingdom, by using encouraging words, bridge building words to connect others to Jesus, and edifying words to feed and build up fellow Christians.

BRIDLING THE TONGUE

It takes a while to tame the tongue, and it's only done by "yielding your tongue" to the Holy Spirit. It's very important to learn how to bridle our tongues though. And we do this by calling on our Father for His help. Repent of the misuse of our words and have faith in Him to help us.

> If anyone among you thinks he is religious, and does not
> bridle his tongue but deceives his own heart, this one's
> religion is useless. Pure and undefiled religion before God
> and the Father is this; to visit orphans and widows in their
> trouble, and to keep oneself unspotted from the world.
>
> James 1:26-27 (NKJ)

> "Not what goes into the mouth defiles a man; but what
> comes out of the mouth, this defiles a man."
>
> Matthew 15:11 (NKJ)

Steps to learn in order to bridle the tongue:

1. *Pause and collect your thoughts before speaking.* Ask yourself for what purpose are you speaking: to build up or to tear down?

> So then, my beloved brethren, let every man be swift to
> hear, slow to speak, slow to wrath, for the wrath of man
> does not produce the righteousness of God.
>
> James 1:19-20 (NKJ)

Death and life are in the power of the tongue, and those who love it will eat its fruit.

Proverbs 18:21 (NKJ)

Whoever guards his mouth and tongue keeps his soul from troubles.

Proverbs 21:23 (NKJ)

In the multitude of words sin is not lacking, but he who restrains his lips is wise.

Proverbs 10:19 (NKJ)

It is our responsibility to restrain our lips! Or as I used to hear Mom tell me all the time, "Zip your lip!"

He who has knowledge spares his words, and a man of understanding is of a calm spirit. Even a fool is counted wise when he holds his peace; when he shuts his lips, he is considered perceptive.

Proverbs 17:27-28 (NKJ)

Learn to listen to what they are saying before responding!

He who answers a matter before he hears it, it is folly and shame to him.

Proverbs 18:13 (NKJ)

2. *Ponder your response.* Think before you speak. What kind of thinker are you? Here are four types: Thinks Before, Thinks While, Thinks After, and Never Thinks. We should try to be the one who thinks before speaking. We not only think in our minds but we also think in our hearts. We should try to give answers from the bottom of our hearts for out of the abundance of the heart your mouth speaks. Let your converted heart tell your renewing minds what to say.

But Mary kept all these things and pondered them in her heart.

Luke 2:19 (NKJ)

And Jesus, perceiving the thought of their heart, took a little child and set him by Him,

Luke 9:47 (NKJ)

But Jesus, knowing their thoughts, said, "Why do you think evil in your hearts?"

Matthew 9:4 (NKJ)

For out of the heart proceed evil thoughts, murders, adulteries, fornications, thefts, false witness, blasphemies.

Matthew 15:19 (NKJ)

For the word of God is living and powerful, and sharper than any two-edged sword, piercing even to the division of soul and spirit, and of joints and marrow, and is a discerner of the thoughts and intents of the heart.

Hebrews 4:12 (NKJ)

3. *Pray!*

I desire therefore that the men pray everywhere, lifting up holy hands, without wrath and doubting.

1 Timothy 2:8 (NKJ)

Therefore I exhort first of all that supplications, prayers, intercessions, and giving of thanks be made for all men.

1 Timothy 2:1 (NKJ)

Make it a habit and a desire of your own to come into the presence of the Lord each morning so He can touch you, search your heart, and cleanse you. Lay all your insecurity at His cross, lay all your troubles at the cross, and surrender everything to Him.

Behold I tell you a mystery: We shall not all sleep, but we shall all be changed – in a moment, in the twinkling of an eye, at the last trumpet. For the trumpet will sound, and the dead will be raised incorruptible, and we shall be changed.

1 Corinthians 15:51-52 (NKJ)

In the year that King Uzziah died, I saw the Lord sitting on a throne, high and lifted up, and the train of His robe filled the temple. Above it stood seraphim; each one had six wings; with two he covered his face, with two he covered his feet, and with two he flew. And one cried to another and said,

"Holy, holy, holy is the Lord of hosts;
The whole earth is full of His glory!"
And the posts of the door were shaken
by the voice of him who cried out,
and the house was filled with smoke. So I said:
"Woe is me, for I am undone!
Because I am a man of unclean lips
And I dwell in the midst of a people of unclean lips;
For my eyes have seen the King,
The Lord of hosts."
Then one of the seraphim flew to me,
having in his hand a live coal which he had
taken with the tongs from the alter.
And he touched my mouth with it, and said:
"Behold, this has touched your lips;
Your iniquity is taken away,
And your sin is purged."
Also I heard the voice of the Lord saying:
"Whom shall I send,
And who will go for Us?"
Then I said: "Here am I! Send me."
And He said, "Go, and tell this people:
Keep on hearing, but do not understand;

Keep on seeing, but do not perceive.
Make the heart of this people dull,
And their ears heavy,
And shut their eyes;
Lest they see with their eyes,
And hear with their ears,
And understand with their heart,
And return and be healed."

Isaiah 6:1-9 (NKJ)

How much longer will we wallow in the sins of the world before we come to His truth and return to Him? Life is offered to anyone who accepts Jesus and turns from their worldly ways and walks in the Kingdom Ways!

The hard work has already been done for us. Jesus took our sins on Himself and died on the cross, and Father raised Him from the grave and He ascended to heaven. Jesus sits on His throne and makes intercession for us to our Father. He has reconciled us with our Father by the shedding of His blood on the cross. All we have to do is believe this to be the truth and surrender to the King asking Him to come into our hearts and wash all our sins away. Ask Him to open understanding of the word in the Bible and show you how to live the Kingdom Way.

And He said to me, "It is done! I am the Alpha and the Omega, the Beginning and the End. I will give of the fountain of the water of life freely to him who thirsts. He who overcomes shall inherit all things, and I will be his God and he shall be My son." "But the cowardly, unbelieving, abominable, murderers, sexually immoral, sorcerers, idolaters, and all liars shall have their part in the lake which burns with fire and brimstone, which is the second death."

Revelation 21:6-8 (NKJ)

"Behold, I am coming quickly! Blessed is he who keeps the words of the prophecy of this book."

Revelation 22:7 (NKJ)

"And behold, I am coming quickly, and My reward is with Me, to give to everyone according to his works."

Revelation 22:12 (NKJ)

Do not be deceived by the enemy whose goal is your destruction. Believe in the word of God. The time is short and the workers are few. He is coming quickly!

THE POWER OF GOD'S WORD

When we read the Bible, we are literally feeding our spirit. God's spoken word brings creation and transformation and still has the same power today as it always has! It does not change.

In the beginning was the Word, and the Word was with God, and the Word was God. He was in the beginning with God. All things were made through Him, and without Him nothing was made that was made.

John 1:1-3 (NKJ)

For the word of God is living and powerful, and sharper than any two-edged sword, piercing even to the division of soul and spirit, and of joints and marrow, and is a discerner of the thoughts and intents of the heart.

Hebrews 4:12 (NKJ)

It accomplishes everything that God sent it forth to accomplish. That's why it is so important to read His word every day and meditate on it.

So shall My word be that goes forth from My mouth; It shall not return to Me void, but it shall accomplish what I please, and it shall prosper in the thing for which I sent it.

Isaiah 55:11 (NKJ)

Let it sink deep into your heart and have its perfect effect on you. Transforming you from the inside out. Lining your life up with the will and purpose God created you for. Try starting your day out with reading the Bible. Speak the words out loud, allowing your self to hear the spoken word of God, and see how it affects or positively changes you each day. How it changes your relationship with others. How it defeats negative or depressive thoughts by having faith in the truth God says about not only you, but each situation you face.

> So then faith comes by hearing, and hearing by the word of God.
>
> Romans 10:17 (NKJ)

> All scripture is given by inspiration of God, and is profitable for doctrine, for reproof, for correction, for instruction in righteousness, that the man of God may be complete, thoroughly equipped for every good work.
>
> 2 Timothy 3:16-17 (NKJ)

Find your favorite scriptures and make a list of your personal fighting words. Anytime you start having negative thoughts, grab your list and start reading it and stand on the truth of God. See how fast the negative thoughts leave you (or how fast the enemy flees)!

> Therefore submit to God. Resist the devil and he will flee from you.
>
> James 4:7 (NKJ)

We are in a spiritual battle, and it's basically for control of your thoughts.

> Finally, my brethren, be strong in the Lord and in the power of His might. Put on the whole armor of God, that you may be able to stand against the wiles of the devil. For we do not wrestle against flesh and blood, but against

principalities, against powers, against the rulers of the darkness of this age, against spiritual hosts of wickedness in the heavenly places. Therefore take up the whole armor of God, that you may be able to withstand in the evil day, and having done all to stand. Stand therefore, having girded your waist with truth, having put on the breast-plate of righteousness, and having shod your feet with the preparation of the gospel of peace; above all, taking the shield of faith with which you will be able to quench all the fiery darts of the wicked one. And take the helmet of salvation, and the sword of the Spirit, which is the word of God; praying always with all prayer and supplication in the Spirit, being watchful to this end with all perseverance and supplication for all the saints.

Ephesians 6:10-18 (NKJ)

There are way more fighting words in the Bible than I will be able to list here. Fighting words could be a book within itself! I highly encourage each person to gather up their own fighting words to help them individually confront what ever is coming against them personally. And guess what, this list will probably change as the battle situation changes, but God has provided an endless supply for any battle you are up against. Just remember, we are already victorious through our Savior Jesus. If you want to go ahead and flip to the end of the book (Revelation in the Bible), you'll see: We win! We just have to overcome this world with the word of our testimony (standing on our Father's word) and persevere until our King returns!

These are just a few fighting scriptures that I love, but there are too many to list them all, so you'll just have to read the Bible and make your own list! Then start meditating on them and memorizing them to get them into your heart.

- Matthew 5:11-12/ 5:44/ 6:14/ 7:1/ 7:7-8/ 11:28/ 16:19/ 17:20/ 18:19-20/ 19:26

- Mark 9:23/ 11:24/ 16:17-18

- Luke 6:38/ 10:19
- John 8:36/ 10:27-30/ 13:34-35/ 14:6/ 14:12-27/ 15:7-12/ 15:16/ 16:33
- Romans 5:8/ 8:28/ 8:31/ 8:37-39/ 12:21/ 13:8/
- 1 Corinthians 6:20
- 2 Corinthians 5:17-21/ 9:6-8/ 12:9
- Galatians 2:20/ 4:4-7/ 5:22-25
- Ephesians 1:17-19/ 2:8-9/ 2:19/ 3:16-19/ 5:1-2/ 6:10-11
- Philippians 1:6/ 2:13/ 3:20-21/ 4:6-8/ 4:13/ 4:19
- 2 Timothy 1:7/ 1:9
- Hebrews 10:35-36/ 11:6/ 13:8
- James 1:2-4/ 1:12/ 1:17/ 1:22/ 2:17/ 4:7-8/ 5:15
- 1 Peter 2:9/ 2:21/ 5:8-10
- 1 John 4:4/ 5:1-4/ 5:14
- Jude 1:24-25
- Revelation 4:11/ 12:11/ 21:6-7

GRATITUDE!

So many of us have something called the "worldly disease." We get so wrapped up in things and stuff of this world that we totally neglect our relationship with not only our heavenly Father but also our own families. It's extremely important to break free from this self-destructive mind-set and refocus on the Creator and Provider of all things, our Father in heaven. Start by pinpointing your inappropriate mind-sets and develop a heart of gratitude. Learn how to put God first in our thanks. Thank God for everything, good and bad!

UNGRATEFULNESS

So many people in our society feel that they are entitled to stuff or think that they are owed something for all they do. They are impatient, "I want it now," and ungrateful, "Well, it's about time/ took you long enough, didn't it"

> Now it happened as He went to Jerusalem that He passed through the midst of Samaria and Galilee. Then as He entered a certain village, there met Him ten men who were lepers, who stood afar off. And they lifted up their voices and said, "Jesus, Master, have mercy on us!" So when

He saw them, He said to them, "Go, show yourselves to the priests." And so it was that as they went, they were cleansed. *And one of them*, when he saw that he was healed, returned, and with a loud voice *glorified God*, and fell down on his face at His feet, *giving Him thanks*. And he was a Samaritan. So Jesus answered and said, "were there not ten cleansed? But where are the nine? *Were there not any found who returned to give glory to God except this foreigner?*" And He said to him, "Arise, go your way. Your faith has made you well."

Luke 17:11-19 (NKJ)

And the younger of them said to his father, "Father, *give me the portion of goods that falls to me*." So he divided to them his livelihood. And not many days after, the younger son gathered all together, journeyed to a far country, and there wasted his possessions with prodigal living.

Luke 15:12-13 (NKJ)

So he answered and said to his father, "Lo, these many years I have been serving you; I never transgressed your commandment at any time; and yet *you never gave me* a young goat, that I might make merry with my friends."

Luke 15:29 (NKJ)

GREED

Greed is the opposite of gratitude. You're either thankful or you want more. It's the "I deserve more" attitude. We should be living within our means, but an ungrateful or greedy heart will tell you that you deserve more.

You're not satisfied with what God provides.

You're not satisfied with relationships—judgmental.

You're not satisfied with the circumstances in your life.

Getting over greedy is learning to pass the "stuff test."

Then one from the crowd said to Him, "Teacher, tell my brother to divide the inheritance with me." But He said to him, "Man, who made Me a judge or an arbitrator over you?' And He said to them, "Take heed and beware of covetousness, for one's life does not consist in the abundance of the things he possesses."

Luke 12:13-15 (NKJ)

First—*Stuff is just stuff*—The question is, does stuff have you? How do you think about stuff? Do you think that having lots of stuff means you're blessed? Do you think the more stuff you have, the happier you will be, or that your happiness depends on getting more stuff?

Second—*Stuff is just a test*—What are you going to do with your stuff? What do you do with other's stuff?

You shall not covet your neighbors wife, and you shall not desire your neighbors house, his field, his male servant, his female servant, his ox, his donkey, or anything that is your neighbors.

Deuteronomy 5:21 (NKJ)

We must learn to be grateful for what we have. Coveting is actually a form of lust. It's a process of setting your heart on something that is not yours. Take a serious look at your heart and see if there are things that have your heart besides God. Who are you looking to for your needs? You should not be looking to people to meet your needs—God is your provider.

THE STUFF TEST!

Gratitude is passing the Stuff Test. Pride and poverty are two spirits, which war with you to get your focus on your stuff and off God, but remember, "Stuff is a Test!" Pride says stuff comes from hard work, done by our selves, not because of God's blessings. Poverty says we don't deserve anything nice, so why pray to God?

Gratitude says thank you! You don't have to justify anything, just thank God! Success comes from living below your means, tithing, and saving. If you want something for your family, then save until you have enough (which requires patience), and then get it. You shouldn't be putting yourself into debt and hurting your family just to have it now.

Work on cultivating an "attitude of gratitude" by the practice of turning blessings into praise, which will help you avoid taking blessings for granted. Give God the first of your thanks when blessings happen in your life. Learn to be content in everything. When you're grateful, God works miracles in your heart.

> Let your conduct be without covetousness; be content with such things as you have. For He Himself said, "I will never leave you nor forsake you."
>
> Hebrews 13:5 (NKJ)

Learn to trust God with everything. He is our provider, and He has a purpose for everything that happens.

> Now godliness with contentment is great gain. For we brought nothing into this world, and it is certain we can carry nothing out. And having food and clothing, with these we shall be content.
>
> 1 Timothy 6:6-8 (NKJ)

Learn to focus on the good things and not the bad.

> Not that I speak in regard to need, for I have learned in what ever state I am, to be content: I know how to be abased, and I know how to abound. Everywhere and in all things I have learned both to be full and to be hungry, both to abound and to suffer need. I can do all things through Christ who strengthens me.
>
> Philippians 4:11-13 (NKJ)

Better is the sight of the eyes than the wandering of desire. This also is vanity and grasping for the wind.

Ecclesiastes 6:9 (NKJ)

Therefore do not let sin reign in your mortal body, that you should obey it in its lusts.

Romans 6:12 (NKJ)

Why do you spend money for what is not bread, and your wages for what does not satisfy? Listen carefully to Me, and eat what is good, and let your soul delight itself in abundance.

Isaiah 55:2 (NKJ)

Do not lay up for yourselves treasures on earth, where moth and rust destroy and where thieves break in and steal; but lay up for yourselves treasures in heaven, where neither moth nor rust destroys and where thieves do not break in and steal. For where your treasure is, there your heart will be also.

Matthew 6:19-21 (NKJ)

Repent of an ungrateful heart! And if you're looking for more reasons to be grateful to God, then take the time to search out a few scriptures. Here are a few to start with!

Therefore, if anyone is in Christ, he is a new creation; old things have passed away; behold, all things have become new.

2 Corinthians 5:17 (NKJ)

If we confess our sins, He is faithful and just to forgive us our sins and to cleanse us from all unrighteousness.

1 John 1:9 (NKJ)

Blessed are those whose lawless deeds are forgiven, and whose sins are covered; Blessed is the man to whom the Lord shall not impute sin.

Romans 4:7-8

In Him we have redemption through His blood, the forgiveness of sins, according to the riches of His grace.

Ephesians 1:7 (NKJ)

But if the Spirit of Him who raised Jesus from the dead dwells in you, He who raised Christ from the dead will also give life to your mortal bodies through His Spirit who dwells in you.

Romans 8:11 (NKJ)

Now, therefore, you are no longer strangers and foreigners, but fellow citizens with the saints and members of the household of God.

Ephesians 2:19 (NKJ)

But when the fullness of the time had come, God sent forth His Son, born of a woman, born under the law, to redeem those who were under the law, that we might receive the adoption as sons. And because you are sons, God has sent forth the Spirit of His Son into your hearts, crying out, "Abba Father!" Therefore you are no longer a slave but a son, and if a son, then an heir of God through Christ.

Galatians 4 4-7 (NKJ)

Come to Me, all you who labor and are heavy laden, and I will give you rest. Take My yoke upon you and learn from Me, for I am gentle and lowly in heart, and you will find rest for your souls.

Matthew 11:28-29 (NKJ)

Therefore I say to you, whatever things you ask when you pray, believe that you receive them, and you will have them.

Mark 11:24 (NKJ)

Behold, I give you the authority to trample on serpents and scorpions, and over all the power of the enemy, and nothing shall by any means hurt you. Nevertheless do not rejoice in this, that the spirits are subject to you, but rather rejoice because your names are written in heaven.

Luke 10:19-20 (nkj)

For God so loved the world that He gave His only begotten Son, that whoever believes in Him should not perish but have everlasting life. For God did not send His Son into the world to condemn the world, but that the world through Him might be saved.

John 3:16-17 (nkj)

Most assuredly, I say to you, he who hears My word and believes in Him who sent Me has everlasting life, and shall not come into judgment, but has passed from death into life.

John 5:24 (nkj)

Most assuredly, I say to you, he who believes in Me, the works that I do he will do also; and greater works than these he will do, because I go to My Father. And whatever you ask in My name, that I will do, that the Father may be glorified in the Son. If you ask anything in My name, I will do it.

John 14:12-14 (nkj)

Then Peter said to them, "Repent, and let every one of you be baptized in the name of Jesus Christ for the remission of sins; and you shall receive the gift of the Holy Spirit. For the promise is to you and to your children, and to all who are afar off, as many as the Lord our God will call."

Acts 2:38-39 (nkj)

But God demonstrates His own love toward us, in that while we were still sinners, Christ died for us.

Romans 5:8 (nkj)

For by grace you have been saved through faith, and that not of yourselves; it is the gift of God.

Ephesians 2:8 (NKJ)

And the peace of God, which surpasses all understanding, will guard your hearts and minds through Christ Jesus.

Philippians 4:7 (NKJ)

And my God shall supply all our need according to His riches in glory by Christ Jesus.

Philippians 4:19 (NKJ)

So Christ was offered once to bear the sins of many. To those who eagerly wait for Him He will appear a second time, apart from sin, for salvation.

Hebrews 9:28 (NKJ)

Let your conduct be without covetousness; be content with such things as you have. For He Himself has said, "I will never leave you nor forsake you."

Hebrews 13:5 (NKJ)

We love Him because He first loved us.

1 John 4:19 (NKJ)

STEWARDSHIP

The earth is the LORD's, and all its fullness,
the world and those who dwell therein.

Psalm 24:1 (NKJ)

Therefore, whether you eat or drink,
or whatever you do, do all to the glory of God.

1 Corinthians 10:31 (NKJ)

STEWARDSHIP

STEWARDSHIP IS GREATLY affected by how you look at things or your perspective. Do you think about things in a worldly way or a spiritual way? When we talk about stewardship, it covers so many things, but basically, it's putting God first in all areas: giving thanks, how you spend your time, whose advice you follow, who you praise first, and how you spend money. Which is what we are going to focus on. The number one thing most married couples argue about is money. How we steward it greatly affects trust and intimacy, which are a couple of the main building blocks in a solid Christian marriage. Most couples have a hard time even putting a budget together because they can't come into agreement on how "their" money should be saved or spent. But let me tell you a secret: Budget=Trust=Intimacy=Happy Relationship.

Bottom line is, it's all God's money! It's His car, His house, His clothes. And if we truly live a surrendered life, then that already includes all those things. We should be asking Him in prayer what He wants us to do with the money and stuff we were blessed with.

> Therefore I say to you, do not worry about your life, what you will eat or what you will drink; nor about your body, what you will put on. Is not life more than food and the body more than clothing? Look at the birds of the air, for they neither sow nor reap nor gather into barns; yet your heavenly Father feeds them. Are you not of more value than they? Which of you by worrying can add one cubit to his stature? So why do you worry about clothing? Consider the lilies of the field, how they grow: they neither toil nor spin; and yet I say to you that even Solomon in all his glory was not arrayed like one of these. Now if God so clothes the grass of the field, which today is, and tomorrow is thrown into the oven, will He not much more clothe you, O you of little faith? Therefore do not worry, saying, "What shall we eat? Or what shall we drink? Or what shall we wear?" For after all these things the Gentiles seek. For your heavenly Father knows that you need all these things. But seek first the kingdom of God and His righteousness, and all these things shall be added to you.
>
> Matthew 6:25-33 (NKJ)

So there you have it! God already knows everything you need. Ask Him first. Pray His word. He is faithful to hear and answer. God is our Provider.

> There is desirable treasure, and oil in the dwelling of the wise, but a foolish man squanders it.
>
> Proverbs 21:20 (NKJ)

The rich and the poor have this in common, the Lord is the maker of them all.

Proverbs 22:2 (NKJ)

The rich rules over the poor, and the borrower is servant to the lender.

Proverbs 22:7 (NKJ)

Impatience is one of the main reasons we get ourselves in debt. We want everything now without waiting. Instant gratification. And once you borrow and swipe your credit card and dig yourself into a hole, "patience" is what it takes to dig back out of the hole.

Excessive spending equals debt, and it doesn't take long to become a slave to money. Over spending is over spending no matter how you try to justify it. You have to be careful about your motives for spending. Financial decisions are spiritual decisions. Is what you are "wanting to purchase" a need for your family or something you just want? Is spending filling an emotional need? Do you participate in revenge purchases, "If he spends, I spend" or "Because I deserve it" purchases? Do you think bigger stuff, nicer stuff, or more stuff is what makes you happy? Do you get something new because the neighbors got something new and you wanted one too (to measure up in status)? So what do we have here? Greed? Covetousness? Idol worship? Revenge? See how fast you can get turned in the wrong direction? If you feel the Holy Spirit convicting you in any of these areas as you are reading them, then it's probably time to pray and confess to Father God what is being put on your heart. He already knows your heart and your motives. He is faithful to take what you surrender to Him and set you free from it, and even send you in the right direction to change things in your life "when you ask Him"!

ARE YOUR PRIORITIES STRAIGHT?

> No one can serve two master; for either he will hate the one and love the other or else he will be loyal to the one and despise the other, you cannot serve *God* and *mammon.*
>
> Matthew 6:24 (NKJ)

There are two main views here. One is a worldly way and one is a kingdom way.

Worldly Way = Fear, sickness, disease, lack, bondage, limitations. It does not always have an answer, and it does not always provide what you need.

The Kingdom Way = Faith in God's provision, there are no limitations in the kingdom, and God does not practice medicine, He has the cure.

Your part is choosing to follow the worldly way or the kingdom way. You can't participate in the world's way and expect Jesus to work miracles in your life.

> Thus says the Lord, "Cursed is the man who trusts in man, and makes flesh his strength, whose heart departs from the Lord, for he shall be like a shrub in the desert, and shall not see when good comes, but shall inherit the parched places in the wilderness, in a salt land which is not inhabited. Blessed is the man who trusts in the Lord, and whose hope is in the Lord. For he shall be like a tree planted by waters, which spreads out its roots by the river, and will not fear when heat comes but its leaf will be green, and will not be anxious in the year of drought, nor will cease from yielding fruit.
>
> Jeremiah 17:5-8 (NKJ)

> But seek first the Kingdom of God and His righteousness, and all these things shall be added to you.
>
> Matthew 6:33 (NKJ)

What you turn to first is what you have confidence in. We should be making God's way our priority.

> Now the just live by faith; and if anyone draws back, My soul has no pleasure in him.
>
> Hebrews 10:38 (NKJ)

Faith in God = Having confidence in God.

> Now faith is the substance of things hoped for, the evidence of things not seen.
>
> Hebrews 11:1

When you sign papers at the bank to secure a loan to build a house, you can't see the house but you have assurance just the same that your house will be built. You should be the same way with God's word. Do you have to see it to know it's true or do you stand in faith that it is? Lack of the word of God while living in this world is like playing catcher in a professional baseball game without the protective padding and gear on. It's imperative that you stay geared up. Renew your mind daily by reading God's word to learn the kingdom way. It will cause a transformation in the way you think and the way you prioritize your life as the Holy Spirit reveals the truth in His word. Faith is an expression of the confidence you have in God and what His word says. His word should be what you learn to rely on, lean on, and turn to first in every situation. It's a spiritual growing process.

> So then faith comes by hearing and hearing by the word of God.
>
> Romans 10:17 (NKJ)

The more we stay in His word, the more our faith grows. A chair has the ability to support you, and you trust in that ability because you use it so much to sit in. God also has the ability to support you, but do you have that much trust in Him?

How Do You Look at Money? What Is the Truth about Mammon?

There are different definitions for mammon when you start researching this word, but it basically stands for money, worldly possessions, or a prideful and arrogant spirit that rests on money.

> *No one can serve two masters*; for either he will hate the one and love the other, or else he will be loyal to the one and despise the other. *You cannot serve God and mammon.*
>
> Matthew 6:24 (NKJ)

This passage uses the word mammon as a spirit, or idol, which is something people worship other than God. If you think about it, the spirit of anti-Christ rules over people through the threat of not being able to buy or sale. So does this make money evil? Well, yes and no. Unrighteous money is evil, and the desire of money is evil. The love of something other than God, or that you put before God, is the same as having an idol.

> For the love of money is a root of all kinds of evil, for which some have strayed from the faith in their greediness, and pierced themselves through with many sorrows.
>
> 1 Timothy 6:10 (NKJ)

> He causes all, both small and great, rich and poor, free and slave, to receive a mark on their hand or on their foreheads, and that no one may buy or sell except one who has the mark or the name of the beast, or the number of his name.
>
> Revelation 13:16-17 (NKJ)

Riches either have the spirit of God or the spirit of mammon. When you take the first 10 percent of your income and donate it to the work of the Lord, whatever church you're led to tithe at, it breaks the curse of mammon. When you tithe, you are protected and blessed by God. The money or tithe given to the church is used for eternal purposes to do God's work and to increase the kingdom through edification of the congregation and won souls. What do we do with the other 90 percent? Be a good steward. When you are a good steward with what you have, God blesses you with more. When you keep the first 10 percent (tithe) for yourself instead of giving to the church to further the kingdom, it is the same thing as stealing from God. It's all His, He only asks for the first 10 percent for eternal purposes and lets us keep the other 90 percent with His blessing on it!

> Command those who are rich in this present age not to be haughty, nor to trust in uncertain riches but in the living God, who gives us richly all things to enjoy. Let them do good, that they be rich in good works, ready to give, willing to share, storing up for themselves a good foundation for the time to come, that they may lay hold on eternal life.
>
> 1 Timothy 6:17-19 (NKJ)

If you're faithful with a little, being a good steward, He can trust you with more.

> Will a man rob God? Yet you have robbed Me! But you say, "In what way have we robbed You?" In tithes and offerings. You are cursed with a curse, for you have robbed Me, even this whole nation. Bring all the tithes into the storehouse, that there may be food in My house, and try Me now in this, says the Lord of hosts, If I will not open for you the windows of heaven and pour out for you such blessing that there will not be room enough to receive it. And I will rebuke the devourer for your sakes, so that he will not destroy the fruit of your ground, nor shall the vine fail to bear fruit for you in the field, says the Lord of hosts; and all nations will call you blessed, for you will be a delightful land, says the Lord of hosts.
>
> Malachi 3:8-12 (NKJ)

And for those that think you're not required to tithe anymore because that was Old Testament and so were the ten commandments, look at what Jesus said in the New Testament.

> Do not think that I came to destroy the Law or the Prophets. I did not come to destroy but to fulfill. For assuredly, I say to you, till heaven and earth pass away, one jot or one title will by no means pass from the law till all is fulfilled.
>
> Matthew 5:17-18 (NKJ)

> But before faith came, we were kept under guard by the law, kept for the faith which would afterward be revealed. Therefore the law was our tutor to bring us to Christ, that we might be justified by faith. But after faith has come, we are no longer under a tutor.
>
> Galatians 3:23-24 (NKJ)

> For all the law is fulfilled in one word, even in this: "You shall love your neighbor as yourself."
>
> Galatians 5:14 (NKJ)

> And whatever we ask we receive from Him, because we keep His commandments and do these things that are pleasing in His sight. And this is His commandment: That we should believe on the name of His Son Jesus Christ and love one another, as He gave us commandment. Now he who keeps His commandments abides in Him, and He in him. And by this we know that He abides in us, by the Spirit whom He has given us.
>
> 1 John 3:22-24 (NKJ)

> Whoever believes that Jesus is the Christ is born of God, and everyone who loves Him who begot also loves him who is begotten of Him. By this we know that we love the children of God, when we love God and keep His commandments. For this is the love of God, that we keep

His commandments. And His commandments are not
burdensome.

1 John 5:1-3 (NKJ)

When you have the love of Jesus residing inside you, you also
love God and willingly follow His commandments out of love for
Him. And if you look at the commandments again, you'll see that
if you love God and your neighbors, then out of love for others,
you would not want to break any of the commandments, because
by doing so, you hurt others and yourself. You would gladly put
God first out of gratitude to Him and out of love for His church
(who is the bride of Christ), and even tithe to help out and support the preacher and what the church supports because you love
them. If that's not convincing enough, then look at this.

> For because of this you also pay taxes, for they are God's
> ministers attending continually to this very thing. Render
> therefore to all their due; taxes to whom taxes are due,
> customs to whom customs, fear to whom fear, honor to
> whom honor.
>
> Romans 13:6-7 (NKJ)

We honor the laws of the government by paying taxes due on
all our earnings, most of the time without even thinking about it.
As we should honor those in authority, for by doing so, we honor
God. But how much more should we want to help the church
family and the preacher of God's word and missions to share the
word of Jesus, and charities that feed, clothe, house the homeless,
and heal the sick (especially children).

> Then the King will say to those on His right hand, "Come,
> you blessed of My Father, inherit the kingdom prepared
> for you from the foundation of the world: for I was hun-
> gry and you gave Me food; I was thirsty and you gave Me
> drink; I was a stranger and you took Me in; I was naked
> and you clothed Me; I was sick and you visited Me; I was

in prison and you came to Me." Then the righteous will answer Him, saying, "Lord, when did we see You hungry and feed You, or thirsty and give You drink? When did we see You a stranger and take You in, or naked and clothe You? Or when did we see You sick, or in prison, and come to You?" And the King will answer and say to them, "Assuredly, I say to you, inasmuch as you did it to one of the least of these My brethren, you did it to Me."

Matthew 25:34-40 (NKJ)

The Truth in God's Word

All Scripture is given by inspiration of God, and is profitable for doctrine, for reproof, for correction, for instruction in righteousness, that the man of God may be complete, thoroughly equipped for every good work.

2 Timothy 3:16-17 (NKJ)

WHO'S WHO?

THIS SECTION COVERS what God's word in the Bible says about who He is, who Jesus is, and who we are. If we don't grasp a strong understanding about who we are, then the enemy will be able to sway us or try to control us with his lies and half-truths. Many of us have childhood traumas from either: abusive families, school hazing incidents, and even destructive past relationships. We have to learn whose opinion really matters. Who have we surrendered control of our life to? We must learn to forgive the past hurts and even people that may have been used unknowingly by the enemy to tear us down. Once we have surrendered our past and allowed God to start the healing process inside us, we have to arm ourselves with the truth of His word so we don't fall back into that defeated state that our Savior freed us from.

Each section has scripture telling who's who. Take time each day to meditate on the scriptures, and let them sink down into your heart where they can't be stolen by Satan or any of his little destructive helpers. Especially meditate on the scriptures about who God says you are. Then when the enemy puts negative thoughts in your mind about your past or who you used to be, you can say, "Wait just one minute. That's not who my Father says I am now!" And speak the truth from His word. Resist the devil and he will flee!

WHAT DOES THE WORD OF GOD SAY ABOUT WHO HE IS

By You I have been upheld from birth; You are He who took me out of my mother's womb. My praise shall be continually of You.

Psalm 71:6 (NKJ)

And we have known and believed the love that God has for us. God is love, and he who abides in love abides in God, and God in him.

1 John 4:16 (NKJ)

For I know the thoughts that I think toward you, says the Lord, thoughts of peace and not of evil, to give you a future and a hope. Then you will call upon Me and go and pray to Me, and I will listen to you. And you will seek Me and find Me, when you search for Me with all your heart.

Jeremiah 29:11-13 (NKJ)

Therefore know that the Lord your God, He is God, the faithful God who keeps covenant and mercy for a thousand generations with those who love Him and keep His commandments.

Deuteronomy 7:9 (NKJ)

For the Lord your God is God of gods and Lord of lords, the Great God, mighty and awesome, who shows no partiality nor takes a bribe. He administers justice for the fatherless and the widow, and loves the stranger, giving him food and clothing. Therefore love the stranger, for you were strangers in the land of Egypt.

Deuteronomy 10:17-19 (NKJ)

The Lord is my rock and my fortress and my deliverer; The God of my strength, in whom I will trust; my shield and the horn of my salvation, my stronghold and my refuge; my Savior, You save me from violence.

2 Samuel 22:2-3 (NKJ)

As for God, His way is perfect; the word of the Lord is proven; He is a shield to all who trust in Him.

2 Samuel 22:31 (NKJ)

God is our refuge and strength, a very present help in trouble.

Psalm 46:1 (NKJ)

The Lord executes righteousness and justice for all who are oppressed. He made known His ways to Moses, His acts to the children of Israel. The Lord is merciful and gracious, slow to anger, and abounding in mercy. He will not always strive with us, nor will He keep His anger forever. He has not dealt with us according to our iniquities. For as the heavens are high above the earth, so great is His mercy toward those who fear Him; as far as the east is from the west, so far has He removed our transgressions from us. As a father pities his children, so the Lord pities those who fear Him. For He knows our frame; He remembers that we are dust.

Psalm 103:6-14 (NKJ)

Thus says the Lord your Redeemer, The Holy One of Israel: "I Am the Lord your God, Who teaches you to profit, Who leads you by the way you should go."

Isaiah 48:17 (NKJ)

WHAT DOES THE WORD OF GOD SAY ABOUT WHO JESUS IS

For unto us a Child is born, unto us a Son is given, and the government will be upon His shoulder. And His name will be called Wonderful, Counselor, Mighty God, Everlasting Father, Prince of Peace. Of the increase of His government and peace, there will be no end.

Isaiah 9:6 (NKJ)

Who is this King of Glory? The Lord strong and mighty, the Lord mighty in battle.

Psalm 24:8 (NKJ)

The Lord is your Keeper, the Lord is your shade at your right hand.

Psalm 121:5 (NKJ)

The Lord your God in your midst, The Mighty One will save, He will rejoice over you with gladness, He will quiet you with His love, He will rejoice over you with singing.

Zephaniah 3:17 (NKJ)

In the beginning was the Word, and the Word was with God, and the Word was God. He was in the beginning with God. All things were made through Him, and without Him nothing was made that was made. In Him was life, and the life was the light of men.

John 1:1-4 (NKJ)

And the Word became flesh and dwelt among us, and we beheld His glory, the glory as of the only begotten of the Father full of grace and truth.

John 1:14 (NKJ)

For God so loved the world that He gave His only begotten Son, that whoever believes in Him should not perish but have everlasting life. For God did not send His Son into the world to condemn the world, but that the world through Him might be saved. He who believes in Him is not condemned; but he who does not believe is condemned already, because he has not believed in the name of the only begotten Son of God.

John 3:16-18 (NKJ)

And Jesus said to them "I am the bread of life. He who comes to Me shall never hunger, and he who believes in Me shall never thirst.

John 6:35 (NKJ)

"All that the Father gives Me will come to Me, and the one who comes to Me I will by no means cast out. For I have come down from heaven, not to do My own will, but the will of Him who sent Me. This is the will of the Father who sent Me, that of all He has given Me I should lose nothing, but should raise it up at the last day. And this is the will of Him who sent Me, that everyone who sees the Son and believes in Him may have everlasting life; and I will raise him up at the last day."

John 6:37-40 (NKJ)

"I am the bread of life"

John 6:48 (NKJ)

"Behold, the virgin shall be with child, and bear a Son, and they shall call His name Immanuel" which is translated, "God with us".

Matthew 1:23 (NKJ)

"And in that day there shall be a Root of Jesse, who shall stand as a banner to the people; For the Gentiles shall seek Him, and His resting place shall be glorious." It shall come to pass in that day that the Lord shall set His hand again the second time to recover the remnant of His people who are left, from Assyria and Egypt, from Pathros and Cush, from Elam and Shinar, from Hamath and the islands of the sea.

Isaiah 11:10-11 (NKJ)

For even the Son of Man did not come to be served, but to serve, and to give His life a ransom for many.

Mark 10:45 (NKJ)

The thief does not come except to steal, and to kill, and to destroy. I have come that they may have life, and that they may have it more abundantly.

John 10:10 (NKJ)

I am the good shepherd. The good shepherd gives His life for the sheep.

John 10:11 (NKJ)

To him the door keeper opens, and the sheep hear his voice, and he calls his own sheep by name and leads them out.

John 10:3 (NKJ)

Then Jesus cried out and said "He who believes in Me, believes not in Me but in Him who sent Me. And he who sees Me sees Him who sent Me.

John 12:44-45 (NKJ)

For all have sinned and fall short of the glory of God, being justified freely by His grace through the redemption that is in Christ Jesus, whom God set forth as a propitiation by His blood, through faith, to demonstrate His righteousness, because in His forbearance God had passed over the sins that were previously committed, to demonstrate at the present time His righteousness that He might be just and the justifier of the one who has faith in Jesus.

Romans 3:23-26 (NKJ)

Therefore, having been justified by faith, we have peace with God through our Lord Jesus Christ, through whom also we have access by faith into this grace in which we stand, and rejoice in hope of the glory of God.

Romans 5:1-2 (NKJ)

Now all things are of God, who has reconciled us to Himself through Jesus Christ, and has given us the ministry of reconciliation, that is, that God was in Christ reconciling the world to Himself, not imputing their trespasses to them, and has committed to us the word of reconciliation.

2 Corinthians 5:18-19 (NKJ)

In Him we have redemption through His blood, the forgiveness of sins, according to the riches of His grace.

Ephesians 1:7 (NKJ)

For He Himself is our peace, who has made both one, and has broken down the middle wall of separation, having abolished in His flesh the enmity, that is, the law of commandments contained in ordinances, *so as to create in Himself one new man from the two,* thus making peace, and that He might reconcile them both to God in one body through the cross, thereby putting to death the enmity. And He came and preached peace to you who were afar off and to those who were near. For through Him we both have access by one Spirit to the Father.

Ephesians 2:14-18 (NKJ)

He has delivered us from the power of darkness and conveyed us into the Kingdom of the Son of His love, in whom we have redemption through His blood, the forgiveness of sins. He is the image of the invisible God, the first born over all creation. For by Him all things were created that are in heaven and that are on earth, visible and invisible, whether thrones or dominions or principalities or powers. All things were created through Him and for Him.

Colossians 1:13-16 (NKJ)

God, who at various times and in various ways spoke in time past to the fathers by the prophets, has in these last days spoken to us by His Son, whom He has appointed heir of all things, through Whom also He made the worlds; who being the brightness of His glory and the express image of His person, and upholding all things by the word of His power, when He had by Himself purged our sins, sat down at the right hand of the Majesty on high.

Hebrews 1:1-3 (NKJ)

Therefore, in all things He had to be made like His brethren, that He might be a merciful and faithful High Priest in things pertaining to God, to make propitiation for the sins of the people. For in that He Himself has suffered, being tempted, He is able to aide those who are tempted.

Hebrews 2:17-18 (NKJ)

Therefore we also, since we are surrounded by so great a cloud of witnesses, let us lay aside every weight, and the sin which so easily ensnares us, and let us run with endurance the race that is set before us, looking unto Jesus, the author and finisher of our faith, who for the joy that was set before Him endured the cross, despising the shame, and has sat down at the right hand of the throne of God.

Hebrews 12:1-2 (NKJ)

Jesus Christ is the same yesterday, today, and forever.

Hebrews 13:8 (NKJ)

In this is love, not that we loved God, but that He loved us and sent His Son to be the propitiation for our sins.

1 John 4:10 (NKJ)

Surely He has borne our griefs and carried our sorrows; yet we esteemed Him stricken, smitten by God, and afflicted. But He was wounded for our transgressions, He was bruised for our iniquities; the chastisement for our peace was upon Him, and by His stripes we are healed. All we like sheep have gone astray; we have turned, everyone, to his own way; and the Lord has laid on Him the iniquity of us all. He was oppressed and He was afflicted, yet He opened not His mouth; He was led as a lamb to the slaughter, and as a sheep, before its shearers is silent, so He opened not His mouth. He was taken from prison and from judgment, and who will declare His generation? For He was cut off from the land of the living; for the transgressions of My people He was stricken. And they made His grave with the wicked – But with the rich at His death, because He had done no violence, nor was any deceit in His mouth. Yet it pleased the Lord to bruise Him; He has put Him to grief. When you make His soul an offering for sin, He shall see His seed, He shall prolong His days, and the pleasure of the Lord shall prosper in His hand. He shall see the labor of His soul, and be satisfied. By His knowledge My righteous Servant shall justify many, for He shall bear their iniquities. Therefore I will divide Him a portion with the great and He shall divide the spoil with the strong, because He poured out His soul unto death, and He was numbered with the transgressors, and He bore the sin of many, and made intercession for the transgressors.

Isaiah 53:4-12 (NKJ)

WHAT DOES THE WORD OF GOD SAY ABOUT WHO I AM

They shall be My people, and I will be their God.

Jeremiah 32:38 (NKJ)

For You formed my inward parts; You covered me in my mother's womb. I will praise You, for I am fearfully and wonderfully made; marvelous are Your works, and that my soul knows very well.

Psalm 139:13-14 (NKJ)

Do not fear therefore; you are of more value than many sparrows.

Matthew 10:31 (NKJ)

Then God said, "Let us make man in Our image, according to Our likeness; let them have dominion over the fish of the sea, over the birds of the air, over the cattle, over all the earth and over every creeping thing that creeps on the earth."

Genesis 1:26 (NKJ)

For in Him we live and move and have our being, as also some of your own poets have said, "For we are also His offspring."

Acts 17:28 (NKJ)

Before I formed you in the womb I knew you; before you were born I sanctified you: I ordained you a prophet to the nations.

Jeremiah 1:5 (NKJ)

In Him also we have obtained an inheritance, being predestined according to the purpose of Him who works all things according to the counsel of His will, that we who first trusted in Christ should be to the praise of His glory.

Ephesians 1:11-12 (NKJ)

Beloved, now we are children of God; and it has not yet been revealed what we shall be, but we know that when He is revealed, we shall be like Him, for we shall see Him as He is.

1 John 3:2 (NKJ)

Therefore you shall be perfect, just as your Father in heaven is perfect.

Matthew 5:48 (NKJ)

And the Lord God formed man of the dust of the ground and breathed into his nostrils the breath of life; and man became a living being.

Genesis 2:7 (NKJ)

And the Lord God caused a deep sleep to fall on Adam, and he slept; and He took one of his ribs, and closed up the flesh in its place. Then the rib which the Lord God had taken from man He made into a woman, and He brought her to the man (a helper comparable to him)

Genesis 2:21-22 (NKJ)

And you shall be holy to Me, for I the Lord am holy, and have separated you from the peoples, that you should be Mine.

Leviticus 20:26 (NKJ)

For you are a holy people to the Lord your God, the Lord your God has chosen you to be a people for Himself, a special treasure above all the peoples on the face of the earth.

Deuteronomy 7:6 (NKJ)

"You are My witness", says the Lord, and My servant whom I have chosen, that you may know and believe Me, and understand that I am He. Before Me there was no God formed, nor shall there be after Me. I, even I, am the Lord, and besides Me there is no Savior.

Isaiah 43:10 (NKJ)

The Spirit Himself bears witness with our spirit that we are children of God and if children, then heirs – heirs of God and joint heirs with Christ, if indeed we suffer with Him, that we may also be glorified together.

Romans 8:16-17 (NKJ)

You are of God, little children, and have overcome them, because He who is in you is greater than he who is in the world.

1 John 4:4 (NKJ)

Love has been perfected among us in this way; that we may have boldness in the day of judgment; because as He is, so are we in this world.

1 John 4:17 (NKJ)

Just as He chose us in Him before the foundation of the world, that we should be holy and without blame before Him in love, having predestined us to adoption as sons by Jesus Christ to Himself, according to the good pleasure of His will, to the praise of glory of His grace, by which He made us accepted in the Beloved.

Ephesians 1:4-6 (NKJ)

But God, who is rich in mercy, because of His great love with which He loved us, even when we were dead in trespasses, made us alive together with Christ (by grace you have been saved), and raised us up together, and made us sit together in the heavenly places in Christ Jesus, that in the ages to come He might show the exceeding riches of His grace in His kindness toward us in Christ Jesus. For by grace you have been saved through faith, and that not of yourselves; it is the gift of God, not of works, lest anyone should boast. For we are His workmanship, created in Christ Jesus for good works, which God prepared beforehand that we should walk in them.

Ephesians 2:4-10 (NKJ)

Now, therefore, you are no longer strangers and foreigners but fellow citizens with the saints and members of the household of God.

Ephesians 2:19 (NKJ)

No longer do I call you servants, for a servant does not know what His master is doing, but I have called you friends, for all things that I heard from My Father I have made known to you.

John 15:15 (NKJ)

THINGS THAT PLEASE GOD

THE FOLLOWING ARE scriptures which spell out many things in scripture that are pleasing to God. Meditate on these scriptures, and get them firmly planted in your heart and mind. They not only apply right now but also in the kingdom of heaven. Some countries are not allowed to have Bibles at all, and it's highly possible that one day in the future that this country may not allow Bibles. We never know, but regardless, in the spiritual battle we are in everyday (choosing to make right or wrong decisions), you need to be armed with the truth of God if you are to walk out your life in the way that is pleasing to our Father and Savior.

> But I say to you, love your enemies, bless those who curse you, do good to those who hate you, and pray for those who spitefully use you and persecute you, that you may be sons of your Father in heaven; for He makes His sun rise on the evil and on the good, and sends rain on the just and on the unjust.
>
> Matthew 5:44-45 (NKJ)

> But seek first the Kingdom of God and His righteousness, and all these things shall be added to you.
>
> Matthew 6:33 (NKJ)

Let love be without hypocrisy. Abhor what is evil. Cling to what is good. Be kindly affectionate to one another with brotherly love, in honor giving preference to one another; not lagging in diligence, fervent in spirit, serving the Lord; rejoicing in hope, patient in tribulation, continuing steadfastly in prayer; distributing to the needs of the saints, given to hospitality. Bless those who persecute you; bless and do not curse. Rejoice with those who rejoice, and weep with those who weep. Be of the same mind toward one another. Do not set your mind on high things, but associate with the humble. Do not be wise in your own opinion. Repay no one evil for evil. Have regard for good things in the sight of all men. If it is possible, as much as depends on you, live peaceably with all men. Beloved, do not avenge yourselves, but rather give place to wrath; for it is written, "Vengeance is Mine, I will repay," says the Lord. Therefore "If your enemy is hungry, feed him; If he is thirsty, give him a drink; for in so doing you will heap coals of fire on his head." Do not be overcome by evil, but overcome evil with good.

Romans 12:9-21 (NKJ)

Let every soul be subject to the governing authorities. For there is no authority except from God, and the authorities that exist are appointed by God. Therefore whoever resists the authority resists the ordinance of God, and those who resist will bring judgment on themselves.

Romans 13:1-2 (NKJ)

But put on the Lord Jesus Christ, and make no provision for the flesh, to fulfill it's lusts.

Romans 13:14 (NKJ)

Therefore, my beloved brethren, be steadfast, immovable, always abounding in the work of the Lord, knowing that your labor is not in vain in the Lord.

1 Corinthians 15:58 (NKJ)

But the fruit of the Spirit is love, joy, peace, longsuffering, kindness, goodness, faithfulness, gentleness, self-control. Against such there is no law.

Galatians 5:22 (NKJ)

For it is God who works in you both to will and to do for His good pleasure. Do all things without complaining and disputing, that you may become blameless and harmless, children of God without fault in the midst of a crooked and perverse generation, among whom you shine as lights in the world, holding fast the word of life, so that I may rejoice in the day of Christ that I have not run in vain or labored in vain.

Philippians 2:13-16 (NKJ)

Finally, brethren, whatever things are true, whatever things are just, whatever things are pure, whatever things are lovely, whatever things are of good report, if there is any virtue and if there is anything praise worthy, meditate on these things. The things which you learned and received and heard and saw in me, these do, and the God of peace will be with you.

Philippians 4:8-9 (NKJ)

And let the peace of God rule in your hearts, to which also you were called in one body; and be thankful. Let the word of Christ dwell in you richly in all wisdom, teaching and admonishing one another in psalms and hymns and spiritual songs, singing with grace in your hearts to the Lord. And whatever you do in word or deed, do all in the name of the Lord Jesus, giving thanks to God the Father through Him.

Colossians 3:15-17 (NKJ)

Wives, submit to your own husbands, as is fitting in the Lord. Husbands, love your wives and do not be bitter toward them. Children, obey your parents in all things, for this is well pleasing to the Lord. Fathers, do not provoke your children, lest they become discouraged. Bondservants, obey in all things your masters according to the flesh, not with eye-service, as men-pleasers, but in sincerity of heart, fearing God. And what ever you do, do it heartily, as to the Lord and not to men, knowing that from the Lord you will receive the reward of the inheritance; for you serve the Lord Jesus Christ. But he who does wrong will be repaid for what he has done, and there is no partiality.

Colossians 3:18-25 (NKJ)

Therefore I exhort first of all that supplications, prayers, intercessions, and giving of thanks be made for all men, for kings and all who are in authority, that we may lead a quiet and peaceable life in all godliness and reverence. For this is good and acceptable in the sight of God our Savior, who desires all men to be saved and to come to the knowledge of the truth. For there is one God and one Mediator between God and men, the Man Christ Jesus.

1 Timothy 2:1-4 (NKJ)

But avoid foolish and ignorant disputes, knowing that they generate strife. And a servant of the Lord must not quarrel but be gentle to all, able to teach, patient, in humility correcting those who are in opposition, if God perhaps will grant them repentance, so that they may know the truth, and that they may come to their senses and escape the snare of the devil, having been taken captive by him to do his will.

2 Timothy 2:23-26 (NKJ)

Do not forget to entertain strangers, for by so doing some have unwittingly entertained angels.

Hebrews 13:2 (NKJ)

But be doers of the word, and not hearers only,

James 1:22 (NKJ)

Confess your trespasses to one another, and pray for one another, that you may be healed. The effective, fervent prayer of a righteous man avails much.

James 5:16 (NKJ)

GLORIFY GOD

God's glory is how He makes Himself recognizable, and He wants to make Himself recognizable to us. He also wants to make Himself recognizable through us.

Everyone who is called by My name, whom I have created for My glory; I have formed him, yes, I have made him.

Isaiah 43:7 (NKJ)

And one cried to another and said, "Holy, holy, holy, is the Lord of hosts; the whole earth is full of His glory."

Isaiah 6:3 (NKJ)

Who being the brightness of His glory and the express image of His person, and upholding all things by the word of His power, when He had by Himself purged our sins, sat down at the right hand of the Majesty on high.

Hebrews 1:3 (NKJ)

Therefore, whether you eat or drink, or what ever you do, do all to the glory of God.

1 Corinthians 10:31 (NKJ)

But we all, with unveiled face, beholding as in a mirror the glory of the Lord, are being transformed into the same image from glory to glory, just as by the Spirit of the Lord.

1 Corinthians 3:18 (NKJ)

When we accept and receive Jesus Christ as our Savior, the Holy Spirit of Christ comes to live in us. He teaches us through the word of God to externalize the internal existence of Christ through our thoughts and actions. This does not happen suddenly. A life that glorifies God is attained by spending time in His word, and in His presence, and His glory both transforms us and radiates from us.

Questions you should be asking yourself:

1. Will what I'm doing glorify God?

2. Do I desire God's glory or my own?

3. When I help others, is my hope that they will see God in me?

4. In hard times, do I turn to God and cooperate with what He wants so He can use the situation for His good and His glory?

5. Do I call on God to accomplish things that can only be done through His power and for His glory?

6. Do I give Him the glory in all things?

Things That Displease God

Just as there are scriptures teaching what pleases God, there are also scriptures that teach you what displeases God. You should also meditate on these and avoid falling into any of the "displeasing" categories. We are by no means going to be perfect because we are still living in a fallen world. What's important is to learn what not to do and when we make a mistake or mess up or the Holy Spirit convicts us of the need to repent, then just admit you have sinned against God and repent. Holding onto the sin will cause more problems than its worth; besides, God is already aware of it before we are. The more you meditate on the word, the faster you will learn to avoid things that are sinful and displeasing to our Father.

> Again you have heard that it was said to those of old, "You shall not swear falsely, but shall perform your oaths to the Lord." But I say to you, do not swear at all; neither by heaven, for it is God's throne; not by the earth, for it is His footstool; nor by Jerusalem, for it is the city of the great King. Nor shall you swear by your head, because you cannot make one hair white or black. But let your yes be yes and your no, no. For whatever is more than these is from the evil one.
>
> Matthew 5:33-37 (NKJ)

But if you do not forgive men their trespasses, neither will your Father forgive your trespasses.

Matthew 6:15 (NKJ)

Judge not, that you be not judged. For with what judgment you judge, you will be judged; and with the measure you use, it will be measured back to you.

Matthew 7:1-2 (NKJ)

Anyone who speaks a word against the Son of Man, it will be forgiven him; but whoever speaks against the Holy Spirit, it will not be forgiven him, neither in this age or in the age to come.

Matthew 12:32 (NKJ)

Now the works of the flesh are evident, which are: adultery, fornication, uncleanness, lewdness, idolatry, sorcery, hatred, contentions, jealousies, outbursts of wrath, selfish ambitions, dissensions, heresies, envy, murders, drunkenness, revelries, and the like; of which I tell you beforehand, just as I also told you in time past, that those who practice such things will not inherit the kingdom of God.

Galatians 5:19-21 (NKJ)

Therefore put to death your members which are on the earth; fornication, uncleanness, passion, evil desire, and covetousness, which is idolatry. Because of these things the wrath of God is coming upon the sons of disobedience, in which you yourselves once walked when you lived in them. But now you yourselves are to put off all these; anger, wrath, malice, blasphemy, filthy language out of your mouth. Do not lie to one another, since you have put off the old man with his deeds.

Colossians 3:5-9 (NKJ)

Therefore, putting away lying, "let each one of you speak truth with his neighbor," for we are members of one another. "Be angry, and do not sin,"; do not let the sun go down on your wrath, nor give place to the devil. Let him who stole steal no longer, but rather let him labor, working with his hands what is good, that he may have something to give him who has need. Let no corrupt word proceed out of your mouth, but what is good for necessary edification, that it may impart grace to the hearers. And do not grieve the Holy Spirit of God, by whom you were sealed for the day of redemption. Let all bitterness, wrath, anger, clamor, and evil speaking be put away from you, with all malice. And be kind to one another, tenderhearted, forgiving one another, even as God in Christ forgave you.

Ephesians 4:25-32 (NKJ)

But avoid foolish disputes, genealogies, contentions, and strivings about the law; for they are unprofitable and useless. Reject a divisive man after the first and second admonition, knowing that such a person is warped and sinning, being self-condemned.

Titus 3:9 (NKJ)

But know this, that in the last days perilous times will come: For men will be lovers of themselves, lovers of money, boasters, proud, blasphemers, disobedient to parents, unthankful, unholy, unloving, unforgiving, slanderers, without self-control, brutal, despisers of good, traitors, headstrong, haughty, lovers of pleasure rather than lovers of God, having a form of godliness but denying its power. And from such people turn away! For of this sort are those who creep into households and make captives of gullible women loaded down with sins, led away by various lusts, always learning and never able to come to the knowledge of the truth. Now as Jannes and Jambres resisted Moses, so do these also resist the truth: men of corrupt minds, disapproved concerning the faith; but they will progress no further, for their folly will be manifest to all, as theirs also was.

2 Timothy 3:1-9 (NKJ)

STRONGHOLDS OF THE ENEMY

You need to search your heart each day to make sure you have not fallen into any of the "displeasing" ways, which we just covered. If you realize you're drifting that way or the Holy Spirit convicts your heart that you're going in the wrong direction in your way of thinking or in your actions, just confess what you know is sin, right then and there, and ask God's forgiveness of your sins (He is faithful to forgive).

God already knows when we make wrong decisions, and He waits patiently on us to confess it to Him. A conviction about something is when we become aware that we have made a mistake or done something wrong. The Holy Spirit will bring things to awareness in your mind. In John chapter 16, Jesus talks about a Helper who will convict the world of sin. The Helper He is talking about is the Holy Spirit of God.

> Nevertheless I tell you the truth. It is to your advantage that I go away; for if I do not go away, the Helper will not come to you; but if I depart, I will send Him to you. And when He has come, He will convict the world of sin, and of righteousness, and of judgment.
>
> John 16:7-8 (NKJ)

God wants to help us, but because of "free will," we still have to make a conscious decision to admit we have sinned and confess it to God and ask for His help and His forgiveness.

The devil loves unrepented sin because it gives him a foothold to set up a stronghold. Most of the time, he uses shame over the situation, just to get started. If we chose to believe the lies the enemy is coming at us with and fall into the shameful feelings to the point we feel the need to hid from God, then the enemy is well on his way to establishing his stronghold. Another approach he uses is the defensive mode, where you start reasoning and trying to justify your reasons for committing the sin. Maybe because others hurt you in some way, then you try to justify you had the right to hurt them back, or get even, or to be angry, or decide they don't deserve forgiveness for what they have done. And at this point, again, the enemy is well on his way to establishing a stronghold.

Strongholds and unrepented sin distance us from our Father and allow the enemy to wreak havoc in our lives for as long as we are deceived and agreeing with the enemy and remaining in the sin. This is a perfect example of the importance of reading and staying in, the word of God, so we do not become deceived by the enemy and fall into one of his strongholds. When we read the Bible, we gain an understanding of God's truth, understanding we are a child of God, understanding our Father's love for us, understanding exactly who our Father says we are, and understanding His mercy and forgiveness.

Conviction is God's way of correcting something that we've done wrong; it's never condemnation, even though the enemy would want us to think otherwise. If we choose to hold onto the sin, He can't clean it up. And when we wallow in our sin because we feel undeserving of His forgiveness, we are basically stating that what Jesus accomplished on the cross for us was not enough.

> Surely He has borne our griefs and carried our sorrows; yet we esteemed Him stricken, smitten by God, and afflicted. But He was wounded for our transgressions, He was bruised for our iniquities; the chastisement for our peace was upon Him, and by His stripes we are healed. All we like sheep have gone astray; we have turned, every one, to his own way; and the Lord has laid on Him the iniquity of us all.
>
> Isaiah 53:4-6 (NKJ)

> As far as the east is from the west, so far has He removed our transgressions from us. As a father pities his children, so the Lord pities those who fear Him. For He knows our frame; He remembers that we are dust.
>
> Psalm 103:12-14 (NKJ)

BONDAGE THOUGHTS

Stay in the word of God, reading the Bible and meditating on His word, which help guard ourselves against the lures of captivity or bondage: pride, idolatry, unbelief, legalism, and so forth (these are just a few). Our tendency is to get so wrapped up in our worldly activities that we forget what God has done for us. We are humble for a while but if we don't guard our hearts and minds, we will begin to think we are doing something right "for God" in order for Him to have been so good to us (legalism thoughts?).

Christians are held captive by anything that hinders the abundant, effective, Spirit-filled life that God has planned for them. Some of the obstacles are as follows:

- Unbelief—which hinders knowing God

- Pride—which prevents us from glorifying God

- Idolatry—which keeps us from being satisfied with God

- Prayerlessness—which blocks our experience of God's peace

- Legalism—which stops our enjoyment of God's presence

If you have believed in your heart and accepted Jesus as your Savior, then you are a child of God adopted into His family, and you have been set free. But there is still a spiritual battle going on all around us. The battlefield is in your mind for your thoughts. If the devil can distract you by filling your time with all kinds of worldly concerns, he has more of a chance of getting himself into your thoughts and keeping you from having time to read the word of God. But if you make time each day to meditate on the word of God, the enemy has less of a chance to affect your thoughts because you will more easily recognize the lies and rebuke them in the name of Jesus. Fill your mind with the truth to stay free from bondage.

Now the Lord is the Spirit; and where the Spirit of the Lord is, there is liberty. (freedom)

2 Corinthians 3:17 (NKJ)

And you shall know the truth, and the truth shall make you free.

John 8:32 (NKJ)

Fasting is another way to break bondages of the enemy and purge you in order to draw closer to God. It involves pulling back from worldly things and concentrating on God. Drawing closer to Him to receive answers and to hear Him clearly. Drawing closer in order to seek His direction for our lives. We should be humble in our approach and not boast about the fast itself but truly desire to pull closer to our heavenly Father.

Is this not the fast that I have chosen: To loose the bonds of wickedness, to undo the heavy burdens, to let the oppressed go free, and that you break every yoke? Is it not to share your bread with the hungry, and that you bring to your house the poor who are cast out; when you see the naked, that you cover him, and not hide yourself from your own flesh? Then your light shall break forth like the morning, your healing shall spring forth speedily, and your right-eousness shall go before you; the glory of the Lord shall be your rear guard. Then you shall call, and the Lord will answer; you shall cry, and He will say, "Here I am." If you take away the yoke from your midst, the pointing of the finger, and speaking wickedness, if you extend your soul to the hungry and satisfy the afflicted soul, then your light shall dawn in the darkness, and your darkness shall be as the noonday. The Lord will guide you continually, and sat-isfy your soul in drought, and strengthen your bones; you shall be like a watered garden, and like a spring of water, whose waters do not fail. Those from among you shall build the old waste places; you shall raise up the foundations of many generations; and you shall be called the Repairer of the Breach, The Restorer of Streets to Dwell In.

Isaiah 58:6-12 (NKJ)

You're Free in the Name of Jesus!

Therefore if the Son makes you free,
You shall be free indeed.

John 8:36 (NKJ)

YOU ARE FREE to follow Jesus in all His examples He gave and all the ways He instructed us in His word and in the ways the Father leads us through the Holy Spirit. I'm so thankful for God's love and everything that Jesus accomplished on the cross for us. I am also thankful for the Holy Spirit. He is the most humble best friend you could have. He speaks things Father wants us to know, He reminds us what Jesus said, He makes intersession for us according to the will of God, He fills our hearts with the love of God, and He even helps us in our understanding of different situations we are involved in (discernment) and with the right things to say.

Nevertheless I tell you the truth. It is to your advantage that I go away; for if I do not go away, the Helper will not come to you; but if I depart, I will send Him to you.

John 16:7 (NKJ)

The Holy Spirit is faithful to do the will of God in our lives. I had been praying for insight on how to wrap this book up and a way was provided. I was in my office working and a friend just happened to stop in to chat. They were sharing a story about their child coming home from school discussing current events going on in the world today. The topic was about the right to pray in school and the potential of "In God We Trust" being removed from paper currency. And this discussion led back to the fact that, in everything we are facing in this world today, there is a choice to be made. We will either decide to get up in arms and defensive through a worldly view of what is going on. Or we will look at each situation through a kingdom of God perspective and seek God for the truth. The truth revealed in this conversation was that no one can truly take the right of prayer from us and the only change is the way we pray. Prayer does not have to involve everyone, believers and non-believers; it can be an individual choice. We can actually speak to God anytime and anywhere because He knows all our thoughts about Him and our situation before we even ask Him. As far as the money issue goes, it's not really about what the money looks like, but it's about how we look at money. It's about the way we appropriately steward the money God has blessed us with and utilize it for His glory.

You are led by what your heart is attached to. If you don't become attached to worldly things, then they do not have control over you. When you are attached to Jesus in your heart, His Holy Spirit will change your perspective about worldly possessions. You still need food and clothes and a car, but not at the cost in value of hurting others. You should be focused on loving Jesus and others more than your possessions. You need food but don't love it to the point of damaging the temple of the Holy Spirit (your body), thus hindering His work through you. You need clothes and shoes, but you don't love them so much that you spend all your money coveting them and not tithing to the church and charities to help people in need. We should become good stewards of the resources He blesses us with: money, time, talent, spiritual gifts, and fruits of the Spirit.

The enemy has a strategy that's working on a multitude of people. He keeps us so sidetracked and wrapped up in the current world issues that he's distracting us from the true purpose God has for us. It's not a "new concept"; it's just a new generation. The closer we get to our King's return, the more trials and tribulations we will go through. That means we should strive to remain focused on Him and His commandments. The most import being, first, "You shall love the Lord your God with all your heart, with all your soul, and with all your mind," and second, "You shall love your neighbor as yourself." True love is when the wants and needs of others become more important than our own. That is the heart of a true citizen of the Kingdom.

If we don't stay focused on His word and have faith in it, we will be deceived, distracted, led astray, causing hardening of the heart, and turning against one another instead of loving and helping each other. We will become an angry and judgmental generation. Does that sound anything like what the fruits of the Spirit bring or is it more in line with the spirit of the anti-Christ?

"Do business till I come." It's a matter of staying focused on what God says and where He directs our paths so we are not lead astray. Even if prayer is forbidden, or Bibles are forbidden, or our ability to buy and sale is restricted, you should remain focused on the kingdom way and follow God's word. Do not get so wrapped up in what the world is doing that you are sidetracked from the purpose God has for you. Continue to do Kingdom of God business until the King returns. Testify about Jesus and the word of God, bring in the lost, feed the hungry, and protect the children and widows. There is a whole list of works you can accomplish and good fruit you can bear for the kingdom. Forgive and let things go. God is the righteous judge, not us. Meditate on the word of God so much that it is written on your heart (memorize His word; we may not always physically have access to the word of God).

Study the Kingdom of God way of doing things. What you are reading here covers some of the basics to kick start spiritual growth. Once you start getting the basics down and continue building a closer relationship with Father, He will take you into a deeper understanding of His word. He will direct your path to the purpose He has for you. We are in this world, but we are not of this world. We are citizens of the Kingdom of God.

As you study and meditate on the word of God by reading the Bible, He causes transformation to take place within you. You become more like Jesus in all His merciful, forgiving, loving ways. He lives through you from your heart. Look through His eyes when you see people and the world around you. You are truly free in the name of Jesus. You no longer have a reason to fear anything. When the devil looks at you, he sees Jesus and the glory of our Father, and he flees!

Hallelujah! Glory be to our Abba, Father!

But be doers of the word, and not hearers only,
Deceiving yourselves.

James 1:22 (NKJ)

Then He said to His disciples,
"The harvest truly is plentiful, but the laborers are few."

Matthew 9:37 (NKJ)

Will you be a doer of His word?

Will you be a laborer for the Lord?

Then go forth and bear much fruit for the Kingdom!

MY CLOSING PRAYER
FOR YOU

ABBA, FATHER, JESUS, my King and Savior, Holy Spirit, my friend, I pray that you open the hearts of each person reading this book so that they may hear what You are speaking to them through these words. I pray that Your Holy Spirit lead them to surrender their life to Jesus and that He in turn cause the transformation that only You can cause to happen. I pray that each person is drawn closer to You and into the personal relationship with You that You desire to have with them. I pray that each person has their spiritual eyes and spiritual ears opened to hear Your word, understand Your word, see the truth in Your word, and follow the perfect will and purpose You have for their lives to bring You honor and glory Father. May their lives and their families be abundantly blessed by the reading of this book, and may it accomplish everything that You created and inspired it to accomplish. May their lives be enriched and bring them inspiration to live their lives as true citizens of Your kingdom. May they see others as through the eyes of Jesus with His love, mercy, grace, understanding, and patience. May they be doers of Your word and not just hearers only. May they be labors for You, ambassadors for Christ, and bear much fruit for Your kingdom! It's in Jesus's mighty name, I pray. Amen.

PRAYER OF SALVATION

THERE IS NO official prayer of salvation in the Bible that you can quote or repeat. The basis for the prayer is implied in Romans 10:9-10 and only requires you to believe in your heart the truth the Bible speaks about Jesus and confess your belief with your mouth or speak it out loud and then profess your acceptance of Christ as your Savior to others.

> That if you confess with your mouth the Lord Jesus and believe in our heart that God has raised Him from the dead, you will be saved. For with the heart one believes unto righteousness, and with the mouth confession is made unto salvation.
>
> Romans 10:9-10 (NKJ)

It's an important step to make, a life or death decision, and you should be proud to shout it from the rooftops! If you're not sure exactly how or when you were saved or just not sure in your heart that you really are saved then by all means, do not wait a day longer to say the prayer below or use your own words to pray to Him. The way you say it isn't what's important; it's the steps lined out by the word of God in Romans chapter 10. Confess with your mouth that Jesus is your Lord and Savior, believe in your heart that God raised Him from the dead, and you will be saved. Believe, receive, confess, and profess.

I went many years being deceived by the enemy. Thinking I was saved. But as I look back, I can clearly see I was not living right, and I certainly was not living my life by the fruits of the Spirit, which are love, joy, peace, longsuffering, kindness, goodness, faithfulness, gentleness, and self-control. I knew who He was and went to church like I knew I was supposed to (every once in a while if I could work it into my schedule), but I had not truly accepted and surrendered in my heart. Then one morning, I felt that stirring inside which was the conviction of the Holy Spirit, and I fell to my knees in surrender to my King Jesus and confessed out loud my belief and surrender to Him, and I experienced what it feels like to have hundreds of pounds of weight (sins and burdens) lifted from me in an instant. There was no denying what happened, I felt truly free for the first time. I felt His love for me, and I felt His total acceptance. Even if you know you were saved and have gone astray by so many sins, and you feel guilt, shame, and generally unworthy (which is what the devil will make you feel to keep you a slave to him), Jesus wants you to surrender all to Him and He will clean you up. Nothing is too big for Him. Return to Him and He will return to you. It's not too late as long as you're on this side of the grave.

Surrendering to Jesus is about changing from an independency to becoming dependent on Him. It's giving up your self-righteousness and becoming righteous in Christ. Giving up your dependence on the world system and becoming dependent on the Creator of the Universe (of everything). It seems like you're giving up a lot, but you're really becoming free in the name of Jesus. When you surrender everything to Jesus, it frees you from the control that the world has on you. You are free to be a child of God as He created you to be. You're truly free to love without fear and in total faith of Your Father. Worldly possessions will come and go, they do not last forever, and you certainly cannot take them with you when you die. But the personal relationship you build with God and His children (your brothers and sisters in Christ) literally lasts forever!

Here is a sample prayer:

> *Dear, God in heaven, I come to You in the name of Jesus. I acknowledge to You that I am a sinner, and I need Your forgiveness. I believe that Your only begotten Son Jesus Christ shed His blood on the cross and died for my sins, and I am now willing to turn from my sin. You said in Your Holy Word that if we confess the Lord Jesus and believe in our hearts that God raised Jesus from the dead, we shall he saved. Right now, I confess Jesus as the Lord of my soul. With my heart, I believe that God raised Jesus from the dead. This very moment, I accept Jesus Christ as my Savior, and according to His word, right now, I am saved. Thank you God for Your mercy and grace, which have saved me from my sins. Thank You Jesus for the price You paid for me. Lord Jesus, transform my life so that I bring glory and honor to You alone and not myself. Thank You Jesus for dying for me and giving me eternal life. In Jesus's name, I pray. Amen.*

If you just said this prayer and you meant it with all your heart, then I believe you just got saved. If you just decided to rededicate your life to Him, this also applies: Your old self is dead, and Jesus has made you new again. The first step is praying for God to lead you to a church where He wants you to be fed. Get into a Bible-based church where you feel led to be, and study God's word.

As He leads you, you will want to become water-baptized. Even if you have been baptized as a child, you have just taken the step to accept Jesus, dying to your old ways and agreeing to walk as a new creation in Christ. By accepting Jesus Christ, you are baptized in the Spirit of Christ, but it is through water baptism that you show your obedience to the Lord. Water baptism is a symbol of your salvation from the dead self you once were. Water baptism represents you dying to your old self and being buried (as you go under the water) and being raised again (as you come out of the water, washed clean) to walk a new life with the Lord Jesus Christ. He has redeemed us for a price, through His death on the cross, and His resurrection, and the shedding of His blood for us! Thank you Lord Jesus!